UNDERSTANDING THE MULTIFACETED MANAGEMENT PROBLEMS OF REFUGEE RESETTLEMENT IN THE UNITED STATES OF AMERICA

The Only War that the United States Is Unlikely to Win

by

Prof. Justin B. Mudekereza

DORRANCE
PUBLISHING CO
EST. 1920
PITTSBURGH, PENNSYLVANIA 15238

Dorrance Publishing Co
585 Alpha Drive
Pittsburgh, PA 15238
Visit our website at *www.dorrancebookstore.com*

ISBN: 978-1-4809-5724-4
eISBN: 978-1-4809-5747-3

UNDERSTANDING THE MULTIFACETED MANAGEMENT PROBLEMS OF REFUGEE RESETTLEMENT IN THE UNITED STATES OF AMERICA (CASE OF SAN DIEGO, CALIFORNIA)

The first question which the priest and the Levite asked was:
"If I stop to help this man, what will happen to me?"
But... the Good Samaritan reversed the question:
"If I do not stop to help this man, what will happen to him?"
(Martin Luther King, Jr.)

"The bitterness of the truth does not affect its worthiness to be said &
known by others"
(Prof. Justin B. Mudekereza)

FOREWORD

Throughout its history, the United States of America has been the home for those seeking refuge from the storms of religious and political persecution. As historian Will Durant expressed, "For men came across the sea not merely to find new soil for their plows but to win freedom for their souls, to think and speak and worship as they would."

In 1883, Emma Lazarus, a Jewish woman in New York City who had worked to help Russian Jewish refugees detained by immigration officials on Ward's Island, penned the poem, The New Colossus, for a fundraiser to construct the pedestal for the Statue of Liberty. In 1903, after Lazarus' death, the final lines of the poem were affixed to a plaque and placed on the pedestal of the Statue of Liberty:

> "Give me your tired, your poor,
> Your huddled masses yearning to breathe free,
> The wretched refuse of your teeming shore.
> Send these, the homeless, tempest-tost to me,
> I lift my lamp beside the golden door!"

For many, America has been the land of opportunity and freedom – it truly has been the "golden door" leading to a better life. Mormons believe that, in 600 B.C., a Jewish family fled Jerusalem to escape pending occupation by the Babylonians. Upon arriving on the American continent – the "promised land" – the family's father and patriarch, Lehi, exclaimed, "the Lord hath covenanted this land unto me, and to my children forever, and also all those who should be led out of other countries by the hand of the Lord. Wherefore, I, Lehi, prophesy according to the workings of the Spirit which is in me, that there shall none come into this land save they shall be brought by the hand of the Lord." (Book of Mormon, 2 Nephi 1:5-6).

Pilgrims, Puritans, Protestants, Jews, Tibetan Buddhists – over the years, thousands have sought religious freedom in America. Likewise, in the past century, people have fled war-ravaged lands in Laos, Cambodia, Vietnam, Iraq, Iran, Sudan, and the Democratic Republic of the Congo (DRC), seeking freedom and protection under the archway of America's "golden door." Like the "free inhabitants of the British dominions in Europe" of earlier centuries, Thomas Jefferson penned that such individuals "possessed a right, which nature has given to all men, of departing from the country in which chance, not choice has placed them, of going in quest of new habitations, and of their establishing new societies, under such laws and regulations as to them shall seem most likely to promote public happiness." (A Summary View of the Rights of British America, July 1774).

Twenty-five years ago, I spent two years volunteering with Lao refugees who had migrated to California in the aftermath of the Vietnam War. I fell in love with the people – I learned their language, ate their food, and participated in their family and cultural events. I met individuals whose family members were killed in front of them, primarily due to their occupation and literacy. They fled across the Mekong River, landing in Thai refugee camps before receiving approval to travel to the United States. Upon arrival, they did not speak the language, knew nothing of the culture, and struggled mightily become education, to find employment, and provide for their families.

Today, a new wave of African political refugees is arriving in Southern California. Many organizations do wonderful work in welcoming these individuals and using available resources to usher these individuals through America's "golden door." However, the conundrum that arises is how to help these individuals and families in the days and months that follow, particularly with respect to education, housing, and employment. Justin Mudekereza offers unique experience and insight into these challenges. He has established and led non-profit organizations in Africa and is fluent in ten languages. He is also a refugee in the United States of America who can provide first-hand observation of both the challenges and needed solutions to help people transition from impoverished refugees into rich and productive citizens.

For Justin and other newly arrived refugees, the question is whether the promise of the American dream holds true for them today. My sincere hope is that this book will "lift a lamp" and provide readers with needed light to welcome these individuals – who are our brothers and sisters in the family of God – through America's "golden door" and onto the path of education and employment, leading to sustained peace, joy, and prosperity.

Jonathan S. Schmitt
President, California San Diego Mission
The Church of Jesus Christ of Latter-day Saints (2014-2017)

CONTENTS

LETTER FROM THE AUTHOR

Dear reader;

The book you are about to read depicts the problems facing refugees in the United States of America, particularly in San Diego, California.

The refugees I have talked with during my study are grateful for the efforts deployed by all organizations and/or institutions and individuals involved in refugee resettlement services. I recognize that a lot has been done to help refugees in this country but a lot more is still needed to be done. Nobody can deny that a piece of bread is better than no bread at all, however if we refer to the wisdom of the King Solomon when he wanted to save a child's life, a piece of child was not better than no child at all (Drucker, 2006). This is about saving at risk people!

Refugees in the United States are sick; they are suffering from appendicitis and they need a doctor – a surgeon. However, we all know that, a surgeon who has diagnosed the problem and who only takes out half of the appendix risks as much infection or shock as if he did the whole job and he has not cured the condition, has indeed made it worse. He either operates or he doesn't (Drucker, 2006).

Everyone in this world is able to save a life; it only takes a heart to do something great no matter who we are, what we have or what our beliefs are.

My request is that, after reading this book, you take an action on one or more of these issues. It will be much appreciated for contributing to the betterment of refugee life in the United States. You can do this by letting others around you know about what refugees are going through in the country, by reaching out to policy makers, by getting involved in one of the areas to make a difference in these people's lives in your community.

By bringing all this to your attention, I have done my job.
Thank you.
Prof. Justin B. Mudekereza

PREFACE

Before enrolling in a PhD program, I was asked by the university to publish several research papers as one of the graduation requirements for a Master's degree in Science, orientation: Project Management. In this journey I accomplished my research papers and got them published. One of the research papers I presented was about "the multifaceted management problems of refugee resettlement in San Diego, California, the United States of America". A few days later friends who got a chance to access that research paper contacted me with congratulation messages and encouraged me to develop it and make it a living book. Their motivation was that a book could help bring refugee resettlement problems to the knowledge of the public in order to help them better. They said that community stakeholders should understand these real problems in order to take actions to address them.

San Diego accommodates the largest portion of refugees in California and the United States of America at large. Since the beginning of the resettlement initiatives in 1975, the area has received more than one hundred thousand refugees. These refugees mostly live in the City Heights area. Despite the many organizations, agencies, and donors involved in the resettlement process, many individuals still face a significant number of problems. These challenges have continued to influence their living conditions adversely. Unfortunately many of the refugees have the idea that after being resettled in a developed nation, they will easily rebuild their lives. However, the reality is far from their perceptions.

This book discusses at length the numerous resettlement management problems that refugees in San Diego continue to face on a daily basis. Among the discussed problems include housing issues, reduction in cash aids, neglect of the elderly, poor healthcare delivery services, bullying and discrimination, domestic violence, lack of information concerning public health and reproductive care, and psychological trauma.

After resettlement, agencies tend to perceive that these refugees will feel more comfortable than when they were in holding camps.

However, with my experience of over 17 years in humanitarian work in Africa and by volunteering in helping refugees for the last 15 months in the United States; I believe that I am among the people who can say how refugees are suffering in the United States, specifically in San Diego, California. The truth in the matter is that these individuals continue to be faced with numerous challenges that prevent them from starting a new life in the United States of America. These challenges need immediate attention from all bodies in the community.

Whenever citizens interact for the very first time with refugees, they ask them a very critical question: "Are you happy to be here?" During the process of writing this book, I have taken time to interview many refugees in San Diego and I also tried to ask the same question (Are you happy to be here?). All sincere and straightforward refugees' answers to this question were always the same: "No, we are not happy to be here; in fact they brought us from refugee camp to a more than refugee camp".

In this book, I tried to find out the reasons why these people had given me such an answer while everyone knows that they receive support from the government, the resettlement agencies, the philanthropic community and many other contributors. I recommend that whoever gets a chance to hold his book in their hands travels a few miles in the shoes of the refugees who are suffering from the problems I have described herein, then stop for a moment and ask themselves a simple question: "What kind of life would I have lived if I were a refugee in this country like these brethrens?". I am sure that if everyone asks himself such a question; there would be solutions to the many integration problems experienced by refugees in this country. I also implore the government accepts refugees to be resettled in this country for one reason: "to help them rebuild their life" after they have lost everything due to war and other forms of conflicts in their countries of origin. I think it would be wishful to think that someone can rebuild his/her life with all the actual difficulties outlined in this book.

However, I must recognize the efforts already deployed and those being deployed by the government, resettlement agencies in bringing the refugees to this land and other donors (moral or physical entities) who help refugees in different ways. A lot has been done but a lot more is still needed to be done.

It is not a sin to repeat myself that by bringing these problems to your knowledge I am doing my part, now it is your turn to do yours and the United States will be a better place for everyone…

San Diego, California (USA), January 4th, 2018
Prof. Justin B. Mudekereza

ACKNOWLEDGMENTS

My profound gratitude to Heavenly Father for enlightening my brain and for granting me strength and energy to do this work. I know God loves refugees and supports them!

A "big thank you" to Dan Collins and his lovely family which I consider as my own my family in the US. Without this family this work would not have existed. May God bless them more again. Dan, remember that refugees will always pray for you and your family for your priceless support to them.

Thank you to Michael and Maryline Staffieri for your love and support, not only to me but also, to the refugees in San Diego, California.

To both Mr. Bruce and Mrs. Kimberly Stinson who have accepted to spare their time editing my book and giving me more guidance on this project; I don't know if it is enough to just say thank you!

Special thanks go to Sedrick and Kalley Murhula for all you have done for me from my first day in San Diego, the United States; Walter Lam the President and CEO of Alliance of African Assistance for encouragements and help at the very time of need…; Rebecca L. Cranor for your invaluable advices and invaluable continued support from the beginning to the end of this project, I just wish I could say more about you in just a book; Adolph Mutagongwa my more than young brother here in the US; Dan Nyamangah; Daniel and Claire Enemark; Bridget De la Garza; June Owino; Bishop Middleton; Deanna Herod; Lisa Clark, William & Jolene Hoevler; Andy Volper; Deans; … you touched my heart in many ways that only a stupid person can forget.

My gratitude goes to Francine Munyerenkana "dulce filii matris meae" for your encouragement and patience; my lovely children Winny Nabintu Mudekereza, Pamela Marie-Reine Aganze Mudekereza, Patricia Mungu-Asima Mudekereza, Benedicte Cynthia Nuru Mudekereza, Angele Mudekereza (R.I.P), Joseph Chimusa Mudekereza, Ketsia Bulangalire Mudekereza and my other children to come…all the Mudekerezas.

In my big family, thank you to my brothers and sisters: Gaudiose Nzigire Bisimwa, Josephine Bisimwa, Isidore Bisimwa Cikwanine, Dismas Bisimwa, Gaudesie Bisimwa (R.I.P), David Bisimwa Byumanine, Bisimwa Kacuka (R.I.P), Deogracias Bisimwa Cirhuza, Jeanne Bisimwa, Leonie Bisimwa, Françoise Bisimwa Cibonga, Chantal Bisimwa Kipendo, Théophile Bisimwa Halinoku, Jeanine Bisimwa (R.I.P), Jean-Claude Bisimwa Mufungizi (R.I.P), Marie-Claire Bisimwa, Claudine Bisimwa (R.I.P), Floribert Bisimwa Nalwage (R.I.P), Norbert Bisimwa Cirimwami (R.I.P), Pacifique Bisimwa Nkolera, Augustin Bisimwa Mitima, Josée Bisimwa Ntakwinja, Josiane Bisimwa Nsimire, Estelle Bisimwa Nabami, Celestin Bisimwa Kujirabwinja, Christian Bisimwa Mulumeoderhwa, Edmond Bisimwa Mutabazi, Beline Bisimwa Ntaburhe, Wivine Bisimwa, Isaa Bisimwa Nyamutumirha, Sylvie Bisimwa Sifa, Brigitte Bisimwa Barhame, Bisimwa Bibi, Bisimwa Muhigirwa (R.I.P), Gorette Bisimwa Bashimbe, Bisimwa Furaha, Willy Bisimwa Balibuno, Willermine Bisimwa Cirubankahiga, Béatrice Bisimwa Furaha, Adeline Bisimwa Rhulinabo, Papy Bisimwa Cirhalwirwa, Patrick Bisimwa Ngaboyeka, Bisimwa Cirhalyamonganwa (R.I.P), Oscar Bisimwa Mushamalirwa. Thank you for your positive thoughts and continued encoragement.

My gratitude to "bene dilectae matri Venantia" Muhindo my mother, the one and only person who loves me unconditionally here on earth; and to my other mothers Therese Musanani, Bernadette M'Burume, Leontine M'Nakalonge, Celestine M'Nyamagana (R.I.P), Cekanabo M'Muliri (R.I.P), Marthe M'Karasancima for who you have always been for me as one of your sons.

Thanks go to my childhood friends, friends, collegues or workmates, classmates and my enemies for no good reason such as: Jean-Claude Kalala, Albert Birindwa, Antoinette Cikwanine, Désiré Mweze, Julienne Faida, Guillaume Bisimwa, Ephrem Tenganyi, Fikiri Maga, Wivine Batudu, Jean-Paul Babone,

Zawadi Bahaya, Adeline Dunia, Elode Cibanja, Gisèle Balyahamwabo, Mastaki Rushingwa, Astride, Beline Bateganyi, Jacquie Komerwa, Wivine Batudu, Akili Justin Cisirika, Yvonne, Théphile Cirhuza, Yvonne Kwabene Ciroro, Adeline, Gisele Baly'ahamwabo, Riziki, Gertrude Cibalonza, Telemuka Naluzige, Jeanne-d'Arc Nabintu, Melanie, Crispin Burume, Noella Namugisho, Sila, Cikuru Rumputu, M. Kasongo, M. Judith, Ndei, Espérance Teganyi, Théophile Ngonyanya, Mirindi Mirhonyi, Kalala Jean-Claude, Ange Nabintu, Philippe Tebuka, Umutoni Claudine, Richard Mukaba, Claudine Mapendo, Telaime Mirhanyo, Guillaume Kashwira, Tuna, Naomy, Immaculate Kiconco, Karume Arsene, Julie Kozibwa, Gladys, Justine, Busuulwa Abdalah, Mack Sangano Makombe, Justine Nabwire, Hadidja, Ellah Wangui, Dr. Blaise Masirika, Mapenzi, Bora, Samy Chokola, Binti, Sarah, Racheal, Nyota Bateganyi, Joseph Betofe, Olivia Borgia, Furaha Francine, Pascal Cirhuza, Furaha Basedeke, Odette Naluzige, Déo Mweze, Lievin Bisimwa, Jean-Marie Cimanuka, Cekanabo Burume, Bora Tumbo, Nana, Eleanor, Bashige Cisirika, Mastaki Corneille, Eloi Cibembe ... – and all those I was not able to list in this book – for your companionship, love and lessons learned from each one of you that might have contributed far or closer to what I am today.

DEDICATION

To my late father Victor Bisimwa Mudahindwa (R.I.P), my best friend ever, who was always amazed by my pregresses in school as a child and always dreamt to see me go far in my life but left this world before his dream became true;

To Joseph Chimusa Mudekereza, so far, my only begotten son for whom I am proud to be father and for whom I have the same dream as the one my late father used to have for me, but a dream I pray to see come true before I travel back home to my Heavenly Father;

To both of you, Daddy and your grandson Joseph Chimusa; I dedicate this book.

CHAPTER 1

INTRODUCTION

Refugees are individuals who flee their countries of origin because of fear of losing their lives as a result of calamities and disasters that strike their homes. The refugees seek asylum in neighboring nations with the hope of finding peace and the hope for a better future. Refugees depend on the international community as well as the governments of host countries to access necessities such as food and shelter. According to a report by the NISKANEN Center (2017), by the United States law, a refugee is defined by some terms that include:

- Individuals who are not the U.S. citizens and need humanitarian aid
- Show that they have been subjected to abuse based on their religion, political affiliation, nationality, or social grouping
- Have not been accepted as citizens of another country and are acceptable to the United States

Current statistics indicate that about sixty-three million people are displaced annually as a consequence of conflicts and other natural calamities. Out of this number, about twenty-one million are refugees. Global organizations such as the United Nations High Commission for Refugees (UNHCR) have been tasked with maintaining the welfare of displaced people. Refugees are expected to receive support in the host country until the situations in their countries of origin stabilize. However, in cases where there are prolonged catastrophes in the countries of origin, a significant number of the refugees may be allowed to acquire citizenship from their host country or are transferred to a third country. According to the U.S Department of State (n.d) this country hosts more than half of the refugees who are transferred to third countries. The refugees are allowed to settle in all the 50 states in the United States of America (USA), and the UNHCR report (n.d) indicates that the federal government has successfully resettled over three million refugees. Zong and Batalova (2017) report that California and Texas have, so far, the highest number of refugees resettled in the ongoing 2017 fiscal year. The researchers further indicate that about fifty-five percent of all refugees have been resettled in ten states including Ohio, Washington, New York, Michigan, Arizona, Georgia, North Carolina, and Pennsylvania.

CHAPTER 2

REFUGEE RESETTLEMENT

Relocation occurs when a small percentage of the refugees is allowed to attain citizenship of a third country as a result of continued conflicts in their home nations. In this case, a third country refers to another nation other than the host country. However, those who qualify for resettlement programs are only the most vulnerable who lack further options. In the United States, resettlement is made available to people who have speedy and a great need for protection. The process of relocation begins with careful selection, rigorous security scrutiny, and intense medical screening. The president of the United States is responsible for giving the criteria to be used in the selection of the eligible refugees (Refugee Council U.S.A, 2017). Nonetheless, the president must involve the Congress in the drawing up of such criterion. The U.S Citizenship and Immigration Services (2016) further necessitates that under no circumstances should refugees be allowed into the country before the president's declaration has been signed. The refugees come from all regions of the world including Africa, Asia, Europe, and Latin America.

However, during my research I have not found any information about how refugees are or can be prepared to go back to their countries. Instead the only option I learned about was that after five (5) years of resettlement; refugees are given a chance to apply for citizenship. This made me ask myself a question: "how sure can we be that there are no refugees who would love to go back to their countries of origin after those five years or later?"

I think it would be good to help the refugees resettle in the country, help them rebuild their destroyed lives and prepare those who want to go back to contribute to the development of their countries. This could be a very good thing for the host countries and the countries of origin of the refugees. The truth is that many refugees flee their countries, due to fear of or, after experiencing persecutions. The situations may have changed after a period of time and these people would be safe to go back home to contribute to the development of their countries...

Resettlement Agencies

In the United States alone, there exist nine registered refugee organizations. They have offices distributed in all states to ensure that the welfare of the newly resettled refugees is upheld. The agencies are tasked with a variety of duties that include meeting the refugees at the airport, providing suitable homes for the individuals, provide essential amenities such as medical care, enrollment into school, and employment vacancies (Refugee Council U.S.A. 2017). These agencies must ensure that the refugees' transition in the United States of America (U.S.A) is smooth and minimal issues arise in the process. However, priority is given to settling the refugees and help in the process of getting decent jobs so that they can receive cash assistance for short periods.

In San Diego, there are four (4) main nonprofit organizations working in partnership with the government to resettle refugees in the country. These are: 1. The International Rescue Committee – IRC, 2. Alliance for African Assistance, 3. Catholic Charities, and, 4. Jewish Family Services San Diego. There are also other local nonprofit organizations and community based organizations working in support to the resettlement agencies' work on the ground. In addition to these, there are also many people with big hearts who usually jump into the process in helping with in-kind donations and/or money to help the refugees. This is the beginning of a new life in the United States of America.

Myths about Refugee Resettlement

While the United States has been one of the largest partakers of refugee resettlement, local people still develop certain negative perceptions about these individuals. The current number of displaced people in the world has reached the highest mark ever recorded. Despite resettlement being helpful in ensuring that the United States continues to build positive relationships with various countries, some of the policies and views about the refugees may weaken their efforts. Some of the biased views about refugees include, but are not limited to:

A. **Refugees are radicals:** Contrary to such a belief, refugees are people fleeing from terror threats in their home nations. For instance, a large population of refugees from the Middle East is fleeing from attacks from extremist groups such as Islamic State and Al Qaeda. On the other hand, Africa has also been primarily affected by attacks from Boko Haram and the Al Shabaab (International Rescue Committee, 2017). Therefore, refugees are victims of such militias and usually flee to escape persecution from these terrorist groups. Furthermore, the resettlement procedure involves the highest level of security scrutiny which makes refugees who qualify for resettlement to be non-radicals.

B. **All refugees are Muslims:** This is the most typical argument presented against refugee resettlement. The United States considers people from all religions and nationalities. Therefore, the illusion that all resettled refugees are Muslims is based on unfounded propaganda. In fact, the International Rescue Committee (2017) indicated that the majority of the refugees resettled in the 2016 fiscal year were Christians and people of other faiths.

C. **Refugees drain national resources:** Despite the fact that refugee resettlement may be an expensive practice, the rewards are also worthwhile. For instance, after the resettlement agencies have found jobs for these people, they become eligible for paying taxes and contributing to the societal welfare.

   Many key figures in the American society such as Madeleine Albright former US Secretary of State, Albert Einstein, Henry Kissinger, Edward Snowden etc. came to the country as refugees, but through efforts and determination, they rose to become significant people in the community.

D. **Refugees come from the Middle East:** Contrary to this belief, the International Rescue Committee (2017) records that a majority of the refugees settled in the United States come from Myanmar. This country continues to be faced with ethnic clashes for many decades which makes it the world's lengthiest serving civil-war. Furthermore, a significant proportion of refugees come from African nations such as Somalia, and the Democratic Republic of Congo, South Sudan, as well as East Asia.

E. **Refugees are mostly men:** The International Rescue Committee (2017) confirmed that more than half the population of refugees in the world are young children. People develop fear on the basis that most of the refugees are men who cunningly want to get into the American soil and cause havoc through terrorist attacks. However, many reports have suggested that children below the age of 28 years are the most affected lot since their parents and guardians perish during these crises.

Apart from the key figures above there are many other prominent people who came to the United States as refugees and made their names in different fields. Among them we have Dr. Ruth Westheimer, Dikembe Mutombo, Dieter F.Uchtdorf, Billy wilder, Marlene Dietrich, Claude Lévi-Strauss to name a few. Dikembe Mutombo Mpolondo Mukamba Jean-Jacques Wamutombo (born June 25, 1966), commonly referred to as Dikembe Mutombo, is a Congolese American former professional basketball player who played 18 seasons in the National Basketball Association (NBA). Outside basketball, he has become known for his humanitarian work.

CHAPTER 3

WELCOMING REFUGEES

The admission of refugees into the United States requires the efforts and collaboration of the private sector, the federal government, state administration, donors, resettlement agencies, Community Based Organization, and individual volunteers from the community. In areas where the refugees are resettled, these various groups may be assigned to them to ensure that they feel welcomed and capable of mingling well with the citizens. Some of the designated groups include the business community, faith leaders, local organizations, philanthropists, mentors, and neighbors. These people play a crucial role in ensuring that these refugees can access public amenities quickly. They also can help them to conform to the societal rules. Different nonprofit organizations such as Alliance for African Assistance is among the nonprofit organizations in the United States that play a pivotal role in ensuring that these expatriates feel welcomed to the country. In addition, the team undertakes the task of ensuring that the barriers towards active participation of refugees in community programs are reduced. Alliance for African Assistance gives training and necessary resources for refugee leadership programs, community engagement, and positive communicating sessions to the locals. By properly welcoming the refugees, they can develop the confidence needed to rebuild their lives.

In San Diego, refugees are welcomed by resettlement agencies that helped them in their travel-to-America process. The resettlement agencies pick them up from the airport and take them to the new apartment rented for them prior to their arrival in the country. In case there was no apartment rented prior to their arrival, refugees are taken to hotels where they spend time as they wait for the agency to find them an apartment. The agencies make sure that the apartment is furnished and that the refugees receive clothing, household items, enough food as well as other things they may need. The U.S. government gives money to resettlement agencies to resettle the refugees in the country. However, there have been many complaints among refugees about the way their resettlement money is managed by resettlement agencies. They think that the agencies steal their money because they don't associate them in managing these sums. They may go buy items and bring to the refugees without knowing what the refugees like exactly and what they don't like. Many of the refugees I interviewed said that practice is not good at all and it makes them feel under estimated! Some of them reminded me just like Gandhi said: "Whatever you do for me without me, you do it against me". Some refugees who went to school must have learned more about that.

Refugees with well-organized communities do not experience serious welcoming problems when they come to the US. Their friends and relatives receive them easily. Only those who are not organized in communities have real problems of this kind.

For instance, refugees from Syria have an organized community organization which helps the Syrian refugees upon their arrival in the United States. They help them with finding apartments to rent, providing household items for their new apartments, and guiding them to grocery shopping, medical guidance as well as orientation to life in the United States. The same effort is done by the Somali community for refugees from Somalia; the Sudanese community for those from Sudan, Ethiopian community, Karen community etc. These refugee community organizations assist only people from their countries. According to me that is not bad because that is how they fixed their vision and mission statements as community organizations.

When I first came to San Diego (in 2015) after my stay in Los Angeles where I landed, I had nowhere to sleep, nothing to eat and didn't even know where to find a restroom. As I was walking on the street after the International Rescue Committee (IRC) and Catholic Charities had declined to provide me some assistance; I saw a building on which it was written Horn of Africa. I felt some relief because I taught at the university in Bosaso Somalia and thought they would help me if I told them that I was in their country and an African like them. Unfortunately, as I was waiting at the reception; the Director came to talk to me and told me openly that he was very sorry to hear my story but his organization assists Somali people only. I felt like losing all the strength and failed to stand up and go. I asked him if he could guide me to the Congolese community so that I could seek help from my fellow Congolese. He answered that he had never heard of any organized Congolese community organization in San Diego.

Refugees from the Democratic Republic of Congo (DRC) have over time been reported to be involved in Domestic Violence and other forms of crime in San Diego, California. These refugees have been unable to unite and make an organized community organization. The fact that Congolese refugees come with the history background of ethnic conflicts has played a major role in the lack of unity which could lead to an organized community organization for the Congolese refugees. Apart from the ethnic conflict background characterizing the Congolese refugees in the US, Congolese refugees who have lived in the country between 15 and 20 years have repeatedly mentioned the lack of support from those who support other community organizations as the major reason why they have always failed to unite and make an organized Congolese community organization in San Diego. They live under a great frustration in a community where other refugees are considered, supported and organized. Those from the DR Congo said they haven't been able to be given attention and support. They face serious welcoming problems upon their arrival in the United States because they cannot find their fellow Congolese easily due to lack of an organized Congolese community organization with a physical address.

In order to avoid being one-sided, I tried to chat with other people from other countries to ask them what they think about Congolese people living in San Diego. Some of them didn't even know that there are two (2) countries with the name of Congo in Africa, which are the Democratic Republic of Congo (DRC) and the Republic of Congo. For my readers who have the same problem about these two countries, it is good to know that The DRC with Kinshasa as the capital city is the second largest country in Africa after Algeria and the most wealthy country around the world... The Republic of Congo, with the capital city Brazzaville is a small neighboring country to the DRC to the west.

Other people who knew a little about Congolese in San Diego area told me that Congolese people don't want to work, that most of them prefer to live on welfare assistance rather than working... I tried to check that statement and I found that it is true there are some Congolese who don't want to work and there are others who are aggressively searching for jobs but cannot find any. From my own analyze, I think that Congolese refugees who want jobs badly are mostly those who lived in the urban areas in their second country of refuge. And some of those who want to live on welfare assistance could be the Congolese refugees who lived in refugee camps where they developed the habit of being given to survive. In the refugee settlements they received food, water, and medical assistance for 15 to 20 years that they lived in the camps.

However, the fact that they lived in refugee settlement those many years and got humanitarian aid does not mean that they are lazy people who cannot work.

All those suspicions, realities and facts explain the need for an organized Congolese community based organization which can help with orientation, guidance and education. This organization, if it existed, could help Congolese refugees in San Diego to understand the necessity to work and support their families. It would be very helpful in welcoming new Congolese refugees and teach them about life in America when they are resettled in the country.

CHAPTER 4

STATE OF REFUGEES IN SAN DIEGO

San Diego hosts the largest proportion of refugees in the State of California. According to Hope for San Diego (n.d), the region settles approximately 3,000 refugees per year. The International Rescue Committee (IRC) launched its operations in San Diego back in 1975. The majority of the refugees at this time were war victims from Vietnam. More than one hundred thousand people have been resettled in San Diego since the opening of the IRC. The main issues addressed by the refugee agencies in San Diego included the resettlement of the refugees by providing essential amenities and issuing legal rights to them at an early stage. Furthermore, refugees in San Diego were prepared and strengthened to enable them to participate in the growth and development of the economy. The resettled refugee youths were also given developmental chances and educational programs that helped them attain the required social and personal skills. In San Diego, food security for the refugees is an issue that is given much priority.

As a means of maintaining food safety, the government, alongside the non-governmental organizations has taken initiatives such as community-based farming projects that ensure that there is food availability throughout the year. Organizations such as the IRC are on the frontline to make sure that people in San Diego help the refugees through acts of donation, volunteering, giving internship opportunities, providing permanent employment, and showing love and appreciation to the refugees on the streets and social places.

However, it has been observed that there are very limited efforts by resettlement agencies and the government in making sure these refugees get enough information on orientation during their resettlement process. They come from the refugee camps in their second countries of refuge to the United States which is their third country of refuge. This lack of proper orientation has led refugees to make many mistakes including breaking the laws unknowingly. When I interviewed them, they told me about how life in the United States has been very difficult to them and very different from the picture they were shown before they were granted resettlement to this country.

When I asked the refugees how lack of proper orientation has led them to making many mistakes, they told me that: "In the short orientation session from the refugee camp, they told us that we would be given (good) housing, that we would be given good amounts of money to be able to survive, that we would be given jobs as soon as we arrive in the country. They never told us that it is not easy to find a job in the United States or that we would take long to get a job. No one told us that we shall be subjected to going to school to learn English language before we can find a job to care for ourselves and our families". Most of the refugees I met said the same things and others added: "we were farmers back home and did the same activities in the refugee camps for the many years we lived there. We thought we could be given a chance to live in farming areas where we could continue the same activities we were doing for living. Unfortunately, we were brought here in a very expensive city in San Diego, California – where there is no land for farming but only concrete. Here we cannot live to do the same thing we knew already how to do. We are obliged to go to school despite our ages and the holes in our brains. In fact, many of us are going to those schools not because they want to learn the language but because they want to keep the benefits by reporting the hours spent in class!"

I continued my interviews with my fellow men and here is a man who was very sick and very desperate in an apartment. When I talked to this man, with my skills in Mental Health First Aid, I realized he was depressed and was fighting anxiety. He wanted to run away thinking that I was a police man but he later knew it was me and he kept calm. What happened exactly to this man? In August 2017 he was involved in Domestic Violence (DV) – child battering and was given a 5 year restraining order. Only a month later he was given a ticket asking him to appear in court because he was caught urinating in an open place. This practice is not punishable in many African countries but it is an offense here in the United States. When I asked this miserable man why he did that, he told me he never knew that it was forbidden to urinate in an open place in the US even when there were no people around. This among other law breaking situations are issues which could be prevented should the refugees get true orientation before and upon their resettlement in the United States.

All these problems encountered by refugees have caused them to suffer more psychological torment leading to, or increasing, mental illnesses. Another one from the most shocking stories I heard was from a 45 years old refugee man who was resettled in the United States with his wife and their 9 children. He also had a brother plus his 78 year father and a 77 years old mother. During another interview, this man told me that he had failed to understand the US system of helping refugees. When I asked him why he failed to understand, he told me: "Before we were resettled in this country, we completed many paper work and pictures were taken for each member of my family; this made me to think that the US government and their resettlement agencies knew very well how many people we were in my own household, that is to say only my wife and I and our 9 children – 11 people in total – but upon our arrival we were put in a 2 bedroom apartment. We did not know that the housing law of the country does not allow this number of people to live in a 2 bedroom apartment. I am very certain that those who resettled us in this country knew very well what the law says about this. The resettlement agency signed a lease contract on our behalf, without informing us about the articles in that contract. In addition to that, they lied about the number of people in my household which later caused me problems since then. I think the fact that we don't speak their language makes them think that we are stupid people and that is why they don't inform us, ask us or associate us in what they do for us."

Findings from different meetings and discussions held with many refugee families show that there were many expectations hoping to live a new (good) life once in the United States. Unfortunately they still meet many challenges which tend to weaken their hope for a good life. Their integration into their new communities becomes very difficult due to the hardships facing them.

With the problems I have observed in the refugee families in San Diego, California; I strongly think that in the upcoming 10-15 years California will just remain the "port of entry" of refugees but will not be the State resettling many refugees as reports say. This is because many of the refugees resettled in California found it hard to live in this state and decide to move to other states after 1, 2 years or even before that. Agencies in San Diego, California know the number of refugees resettled in the state but they don't know the number of refugees who still living here. From those resettled, a good number find it difficult for them to live in California and they move to other states and are not recorded by the agencies. I personally helped many refugee families from the Democratic Republic of Congo (DRC) with rides to the airport.

I have realized that today, no agency or institution can claim to know the exact number of refugees living in San Diego, California. When asked about the number of refugees in the county, the resettlement agencies and other organizations refer to the statistics of refugees who were resettled in the county from a certain fiscal year. They likely forget that every single week or month there are many refugee families leaving San Diego to move to other states due to hardships facing them. According to me, not knowing the exact number of people in the area (not only refugees) is another big problem in development because it is not easy or even possible to plan for development if the numbers of the populations are not known.

The refugees who leave San Diego, California hope that they will be able to rebuild their lives in other states where they think life is a little less expensive and jobs can be found easily than in California. They forget that this wandering can make them face more problems and more suffering. One of the major problems they can face upon arrival in another state is integration in the new community. There they have to meet new people, make new friends and above all face new and absolutely strange weather conditions. Readers who have experience in education will also understand how this change can affect children's education too. The children have to go to new schools, meet new teachers, new friends etc. which can negatively affect their education.

CHAPTER 5

RESETTLEMENT STATUS OF REFUGEES IN SAN DIEGO

As seen from the above discussion, San Diego is home to more than one hundred thousand (100,000) refugees who come from various countries of the world (KPBS, n.d). In the San Diego area, four organizations or agencies are responsible for taking care of refugees. All these organizations are financed by the federal government and private donors to implement different projects in the process of refugee resettlement in the country. The four agencies include Catholic Charities, International Rescue Committee, Alliance of African Assistance, and Jewish Family Services. Other than the four resettlement organizations in the area, other key players help the refugees and include aid agencies, individual well-wishers, business groups, churches and other faith based organizations. A significant portion of the refugees resettled in San Diego is sited in the City Heights Community making it the most refugee populated area in the county of San Diego. A mix of people from all regions and countries can be found in these settlement programs. The highest portion of these characters, however, comes from the Asian continent including places such as Myanmar, Thailand, and Vietnam.

Other refugee populations are found in other areas of the country such as El Cajon, Spring Valley, Lakeside etc. Some resettlement agencies have opened up offices in these other areas to be able to reach out to the refugees living in the areas. The county of San Diego runs different programs in partnership with the Public Consulting Group (PCG) and ResCare which are private companies working as contractors.

CHAPTER 6

MANAGEMENT PROBLEMS
OF REFUGEES IN SAN DIEGO

With the high influx of the refugees in the San Diego region, management is-sues are bound to occur. The management issues arise as a result of poor plan-ning on the side of the responsible resettlement agencies or the economic conditions in the area. Therefore, to ensure that these refugees are well taken care of throughout their stay in the United States, there is high need to assess the current management problems facing them. Afterward, proper measures can be taken to insure that these conditions are amicably addressed.

I went to meet with a leader of one of the four resettlement agencies resettling refugees in San Diego to try to understand why refugees are not given the nec-essary help they need to reduce their worries. This leader told me that they recognize the necessity for more assistance to the refugees, especially due to the increased number of resettled refugees, but resettlement agencies can only give what they receive. I completely understood because even the most beau-tiful girl gives only what she has!

Overarching systemic issue:
According to Claire Enemark (2016), individuals with refugee status interact with many agencies during their second country & third country journeys. Unfortunately, incentives are misaligned across large systems. There is too much bureaucracy (UNHCR, International non-profits, Federal agencies, County agencies and local non-profits) and communication is not strong. This leads to a lack of quality care for individuals with refugee status. That means that second (often neighboring) countries (Uganda, Kenya, Tanzania, Thai-

land, Lebanon, etc) are usually not thrilled to receive refugees and house them. In camps or in urban areas, services rendered to refugee families are very few. Upon being resettled, often refugees "orientation" to the new country & city is very limited. In San Diego their cases go to the County so they can receive cash aid but they get lumped in with many other welfare clients. Each agency has different incentives and outcomes are rarely communicated effectively. In this state of things, the refugees wait a lot and spend much time waiting for paper work processing to be able to access some vital services. One refugee I met and who was a school principal back from his county told me that he was very shocked to see the long waiting at the welfare office. "I lost my hope to be able to rebuild my life in the United States the very first day I came to the welfare office. No case is given priority there, all cases are taken easy and the workers take their time", said the man.

San Diego issues:
Lack of affordable housing, Lack of Decent Employment, Increasing Rates of Prostitution and Drug Use, Language Barriers (combined with poor quality of San Diego Continuing Education ESL courses & San Diego Unified Schools' reduction in support for Newcomer students), Unwelcoming Communities, Difficulty in Accessing Healthcare Services, Problems Accessing Decent Education, Cultural Integration Issues, Lack of Personal Necessities, Transportation Problems Insufficiency of Cash Aid, Bullying and Segregation in Schools and Social Places Overcrowding and Disease Outbreaks, Travel Bans, Mental Health and Psychological trauma, Access to Reproductive Healthcare Services, Lack of Information about Public Health Issues, Increased Crime Rates, Human Trafficking Activities, Neglect of the Elderly Refugees, Domestic Violence (DV) among other issues.

This is by no means an exhaustive list; instead it reflects the core issues that refugees face in San Diego (USA). I believe that all other issues stem from these like symptoms.

These problems are real and they create a greater need for more support to refugee families in this country. This calls for more actions in communities where they are resettled in order to help them rebuild their lives and become true members of the communities. Once they feel loved and given the chance to rebuild their lives they can contribute to the development of their communities and the country at large.

I also believe that agencies must work hard to ensure that every refugee having fled violence, persecution, war or disaster in their home country and comes to this country, particularly in San Diego California, has necessary means of living here. That includes feeling the warmth and love from community members they meet and are called to live with. This is the only way we can contribute to the peace and development efforts and make this country a better place for everyone.

Housing Problems

One major issue affecting the resettlement of refugees in San Diego is the availability of affordable and proper housing. Initially, the number of refugees being resettled was not as high as that being relocated today. The U.S Department of State reported that during the 2016 fiscal year, the San Diego region received the largest number of resettled refugees in the country with a record of an average of 250 additional refugees per month. Therefore, with the increase of these individuals, housing has become a major concern in the county.

In fact, it has been reported that the resettled people are at times acquired an apartment whose space can barely accommodate a single family (Burks, 2014). Besides, some of the refugees were forced to live out in motels as the responsible agencies tried to find permanent living houses for them. Property-owners have also been providing strict housing agreements that require that excess families should pay a higher rent. This has adversely affected the refugees because the resettlement agencies provide only a fixed amount of cash for rent and other expenditures. It is also a fact that a significant proportion of the property-owners take advantage of the refugees based on the ideology that they have been awarded huge lump sums by the government and the resettlement agencies. Furthermore, some of the landlords and landladies feel that these people are a burden to them. Hence, they revoke their application to stay in their houses (Sanchez, 2015). Therefore this rejection leads to the refugees having to stay in clustered places such as the cheap motel rooms or other demeaning places.

The monthly rental fees have also been on the increase based on the changes in the economy. This has forced the construction of housing properties to soar. Therefore, refugees who are being resettled at the moment are faced with the choice of living in shattered shelters that are sometimes unhygienic and bring a lot of health concerns. Resettlement agencies such as the International Rescue Committee have been unable to match the increases in rent to the amount paid to refugees. This has been a major blow on the resettled populations.

Many complaints among refugees in San Diego have been observed in regard to apartment rental process due to the fact that they don't know the contents of their lease contracts. For instance, without proper orientation or information sessions, a refugee from Africa will not easily understand that the rent of a two (2) bedroom apartment can cost fifteen hundred US dollars ($1500) a month, an amount that could build a house in their respective countries. They think the refugee resettlement agencies bamboozled the story in order to steal their money.

Last year, a report from a refugee family mentor working with New Neighbor Relief (NNR) said that on July 28th, National Public Radio (NPR) aired a story about the International Rescues Committee (IRC), one of the refugee resettlement agencies in San Diego. The story on the radio said that IRC intentionally advised refugees not to list every person in the family on the lease. Now, many families are being evicted because of breaking housing laws and landlords don't want to be fined. One of the refugees interviewed said: "How could this happen?"

The law, according to the manager at La Terreza apartment complex, states that no more than two (2) people per bedroom plus one in the living room can be accepted. Landlord allowing more than that is looking the other way. During my research, I met many refugee families with a large number of people who were living in 2 bedroom apartments. They all revealed to me the rental burdens on their families and the disappointment they felt about the life in the United States due to these housing problems. Before the government granted them resettlement to this country as refugees, they knew that most of the refugees (especially those coming from Africa) have many children and other family members moving to the United States with them. It looks like nothing was done ahead of time to prepare the housing of the refugees with large families. This is something very serious. They asked me the following few questions that I was not able to answer: "How do the government and re-settlement agencies think refugees will be housed in these conditions where the law locks the housing system and does not provide any exceptions for people like refugees or other alternatives?" Why are they bringing in refugees if they will have to face all these housing problems?" Can anyone among my readers help with an answer to one or all these 2 questions?

Living condition is terrible in many apartments with large number of people. Hygiene conditions are a big issue. Cockroaches, bugs and bed bugs are seen everywhere in the apartments and the smells in the apartment are horrible! New Neighbor Relief Volunteers and others who visit refugee families as mentors have tried to teach them about hygiene but they cannot do enough because refugees have very limited resources to allow them care for their families and keep good hygiene conditions at the same time!

The fact that these individuals do not have a stable source of income comes from a major contributor to the lack of affordable housing. The latter brings out another management problem that the refugees face in San Diego.

Lack of Decent Employment

Upon arrival and settlement in San Diego, refugees are willing to take any available jobs. In most cases, only manual jobs are availed to them. These only pay them the minimum wage which is insufficient for their family daily expenses. However, the main problem is that despite the time or effort that these refugees dedicate to their work, it is almost impossible to earn promotions. Therefore, they are subjected to the minimum wage even after years of working which is prejudicial and an indication of lack of appreciation by the employers (Garret, 2006). Resettled refugees who are educated and had well-paying jobs in their home countries find it exasperating that they cannot be presented with the same opportunities in San Diego firms. Many employers fail to recognize work experience from outside the United States which further makes it difficult for the refugees to earn reputable jobs. Additionally, businesses also fail to recognize any foreign educational certification from other nations, more so, the developing worlds, making it more difficult for the refugees advance in job prospects.

While at the workplace, refugees also become victims of discrimination based on their nationality. Therefore, employers offer them roles that cannot earn them sustainable incomes. This makes it difficult for them to have a comfortable life as they had expected.

Furthermore, the employers know that these individuals are desperate and will take any duties assigned to them without raising any complaints. The naïve refugees feel that they do not have any rights. This makes them an easy target for the exploitive employers. During work dedicated to a particular team in an organization, it is common to find that the refugees are given a load full of tasks whereas the locals are assigned easy and few roles. The ironic thing is that during payment, the same refugees who toiled throughout the day or month are underpaid. Corcoran (2017) shares her findings that industries such as meat packers and chicken plants are exploiting the refugees in the name of employing them when in fact, they severely underpay them. Furthermore, the researcher finds that responsible agencies such as the International Rescue Committee (IRC) are only contented with seeing the refugees find jobs, but they do not pay attention to the exploitation they undergo. The same poor pay is also subject to taxation because the refugees have already become permanent residents or U.S citizens. Therefore, they are left with little disposable income which leads them to conduct illegal activities such as drug smuggling and prostitution.

However, some efforts to help refugees have been noted by different organizations or institutions but still very few refugees have access to these opportunities due to different reasons such as lack of formal education among refugees, lack of skills, lack of experience required by some job positions, transportation etc. Some refugees from Iraq, Syria and other Asian countries have access to jobs in companies owned by refugees from those countries. They came to the US a long time ago and are already citizens. I have noted that it is very difficult for African refugees to have access to jobs in these Asian owned companies… this might be due to communication problems. This doesn't mean that Asian refugees are not faced by lack of descent employment like other refugees.

Job fair events have been being organized in San Diego and open to many un-employed citizens including permanent residents and asylum seekers who are allowed to work in the country. In these circumstances, refugees have also had very little to no chance to secure a job. Because very few of them are not in-formed about the events and many of those that do get the information are not able to show up at the event due to of lack of transportation. Furthermore, the refugees who get a chance to make it to job fair events are faced by lan-guage barriers and untailored resumes making it difficult for them to compete with the citizens. They end up getting no job at these events!

In order to help refugees find jobs, the County of San Diego through San Diego Workforce Partnership with their contractors such as the Public Con-sulting Group (PCG) and ResCare has implemented some programs in this perspective. The program called Work Experience (WEX) and the program known as Expanded Subsidized Work Experience (ESE) are great incentives and a gateway to helping refugees and other citizens finding jobs. The focus is on helping the employee gain skills or experience they can rely on to re-main employed by company owners while earning an income. For instance, the Expanded Subsidized Work Experience (ESE) allows an employee to get a job and work for a period of six (6) months gaining experience that will lead to full time employment. In this program, the government pays the wages of the employee in a scale that really may be very interesting to em-ployers who hesitate to employ refugees. The employers who employ refugees or other job seekers under the Expanded Subsidized Work Experi-ence (ESE) will have the very first 2 months wages paid off 100% by the gov-ernment, 2 months paid off 50% and 25% for the last 2 months. Under the same program, the employer signs an agreement and accepts to continue employing people who were registered and for whom the government con-tributed on the wages for the first 6 months.

Although these programs are set up by the government, there would be a greater opportunity to help refugees find employment in San Diego, but many refugees do not understand the necessity to take advantage of them. Because these are government administered programs, some of the refugees I met were not really interested to get jobs under these programs. As refugees receive cash aid, health insurance from the government; many refugees fear to participate in the WEX and ESE programs. They think by participating in these programs they will lose their welfare benefits such as food stamps also known as Cal-Fresh, healthcare insurance (Med-Cal) etc.

As soon as we heard about Work Experience (WEX) and Expanded Subsidized Work Experience (ESE), we tried to get involved and worked even harder to talk with company owners and showed them the necessity of hiring refugees through WEX and ESE programs which, as we said earlier, look to be greater incentives in the process of refugees' employment in San Diego, California. Since we, at New Neighbor Relief, got acquainted with company owners couples of refugees who accepted to work full time under ESE program rejected the offer only two (2) days before they could start the job. Their refusal was due to the fact that the Public Consulting Group (PCG) and the Country were involved in the program. They thought that by being employed through this program administered by the County and their contractor PCG they would lose their welfare benefits especially health insurance. Everyone involved was very disappointed because the paper work was already done and the employer had already made special arrangements to facilitate their transportation to and from work. I was personally shocked to see how I fought for these refugees to be part of the program; I made many contacts and meetings with PCG and the employer.

I advised those involved in the administration of these programs to work hard again and make sure refugees are well informed, trained or educated about the necessity for them to take up the job opportunities through WEX and/or ESE because these are opportunities they cannot find elsewhere. Refusing to take up a jobs looks very funny because refugees lack jobs and they have been having serious financial issues due to lack of jobs. During one of our meetings, after the refugees have rejected the job offers because they involved the County and their contractor PCG; the employment advisor at America's Job Center/ECCC said: "Justin, we have enough funding for this program but it has been really difficult to find people interested in the opportunities that it offers". I told them to make more efforts in order to train, inform or educate refugees about the program and its benefits. Just because a program may look great, it cannot help or become successful if awareness is not enough among clients or beneficiaries. There must have been problems in the planning process of the program. I told them there was need to rethink strategies to make sure many refugees can accept to participate in the program. They need jobs badly; they just need to understand how things work with the program so that they can be part of it. Furthermore, clients' participation is always important in the planning process of any program that really needs to positively impact their lives. In this case, there will be no surprises of that kind we saw because all the program stakeholders are aware of how it operates and what are the benefits to be part of the program. Printed material dissemination would be a great strategy to increase awareness about a good program like that in case it was not possible to include the participation of the beneficiaries in the planning process. The materials to be disseminated should be in native languages spoken and understood by the clients for best results.

Solving a development problem is like treating a sick person. If the diagnostic used is wrong, then the treatment will definitely be wrong too. The chance of death of the patient is very high. A proper problem assessment is needed beforehand to know what can solve the problems observed in the community. Just like a doctor who needs to give a good treatment to a patient will be prepared to listen to him first to know how he is suffering. Asking questions such as how long the pain has existed, how/when the pain started and what kind of treatment has the patient tried for the same problem in the past? Unless he uses this process, the doctor will be unlikely able to cure the sickness. Many efforts have been deployed in helping refugees find jobs in San Diego, California but I think that more efforts are still needed. It is true that many refugees are illiterates and they are suffering language barriers unlike other refugees who came to the country with university degrees or other employable skills. Unfortunately, as we discussed above; many employers fail to recognize work experience from outside the United States. This makes it difficult for the refugees to earn reputable jobs. Business owners also fail to recognize any foreign educational certification from other nations, more so, the developing worlds, making it worse for the refugees. This is the reason why I think that this problem should be discussed at another level.

In the San Diego area, resettlement agencies, government contractors such as the Public Consulting Group (PCG), ResCare and other organizations helping refugees have set up many desks to help refugees. They use job search, job readiness and resume building where refugees can learn how to search for jobs, how to get ready for a job interview and how to build a good or convincing resume. If this was really what refugees needed to find jobs, the tens of thousands of refugees in San Diego would have been all employed today considering the number of organizations helping in this process with job search, job readiness and resume building. Illiterate refugees don't need a well tailored resume to get a job and they don't need job interview skills either. What does a bird have to do with a toothbrush or what does a disabled person with no legs have to do with shoes? Many newcomers who studied in their home countries before coming to the United States have skills and are able to build their own resume and can speak some good English for job interviews if it was the only thing that was needed to get them employed. My own story and experience in this very specific matter has shown me what it looks like to find a job in San Diego, California. I came to the United States with skills and a 17 year experience in the nonprofit sector, I taught in universities in Africa and helped many people to build their resumes and they got jobs. Yet when it came to America, it was almost impossible to be employed. This was despite the hundreds of job opportunities to which I applied!

What does it really take to help refugees find employment in San Diego, California? Learning from my own experience; I realized that we only need to mobilize and/or sensitize employers (business owners, organizations, public and private institutions). I know that refugees are also human resources who can work and reach the same results as other citizens. I recognize that it may take some time for some refugees to get used to their work environment but they can make it right after a while. It is just a matter of giving them a chance for equal opportunities.

Here is what we did to see how this can really work. When we were just starting New Neighbor Relief – NNR in San Diego, we had a few refugee families which were referred to us by one of the resettlement agencies. These people stayed in their apartments for about 3 months without going out and without jobs. During one of our visits with Dan Collins, the Board President of NNR, these refugees told us: "We came from a refugee camp to a more than a refugee camp". Because I speak the same language as them, President Collins asked me to interpret for him what they had said. Which I did and he was shocked. When asking them why they think like that; they said that in a refugee camp, they could visit friends and relatives; they could go out just for sightseeing or do some farming labor jobs instead of staying locked in their homes all day long.

Two days later, in my routine meeting with NNR President, I suggested him to give jobs to the heads of these refugee families. This was not only to break the idleness they were suffering but also to help them earn incomes to support their families. It would help them to prevent any mental health issue that could arise due to lack of employment considering the expenses they have to take care of every month. At first President Collins thought like other American employers and told me: "Justin, how can these people work when they don't speak English language and they have no skills, no experience at all?" President Collins owns a painting company called DC Painting. I asked one question: "President, what does language have to do with painting job? Do painters need to talk to the walls they paint or do they talk to the paint itself? If yes, which language do these things speak? I know that you like helping needy people, so are these refugees. Could you try to hire them and ask your foremen to guide them and see the results?" He thought about, he accepted and he decided to hire 6 refugee men in his company to see the results. He did not ask them to submit their resumes neither invite them for job interview. He was just convinced that giving these refugees a chance to work will help them to reduce stress, break the idleness and make incomes for their families. Here it was only a matter of willing to help the refugees in need!

It is now almost fourteen (14) months since these refugees were employed by DC Painting and they are successful. They have learned some English, gained some skills at work and the company is satisfied by the results. Today, the same company has added more refugees who were referred by New Neighbor Relief – NNR and the total number of refugees employed by DC Painting is 15 refugee heads of families. More about this experience can be found at www.newneighborrelief.org or contact DC Painting directly for questions on how he did this. Many of these employed refugees are attending English classes in the evening after work. The next step is to help them buy a car in order for them to go to and from work every day and this will help them become independent. I totally believe that this is what refugees need to be able to rebuild their lives in this country.

President Dan Collins decided to discuss this great experience with other business owners in San Diego, California. He wanted to help them understand that refugees are also human resources. We strongly believe that if other business owners in San Diego can do like Dan Collins did, many refugees can be employed and the process of starting a new life in the United States can become a reality rather than a slogan. Let us suppose that he talks to only 10 of his friends who own companies and they accept to employ 15 refugees each. This action can automatically bring relief to more 150 refugee heads of families.

Dr. Sheila Mitra is a researcher who has been looking into refugee matters in City Heights for over 9 years. She is a very active woman who is driven by a desire to help refugees in San Diego and contribute to global change. I have known her from different meetings and workshops about refugee issues. She appreciated my efforts in devoting my skills, time and energy to the cause of refugees in the San Diego, California. In September 2017, Dr. Sheila sent out an email informing me about her desire to organize a free workshop to teach newcomers in San Diego how to build their resumes and be able to get jobs like others. I replied to Dr. Sheila and gave her my opinion about that. However, I recognized and appreciated her efforts to have the refugees in her heart. I told her that refugees needed more than resume building support to be able to access jobs in San Diego. With the courage of this lady and her willingness to help the refugees, I believe she could develop some strategies and implement them to help while keeping the idea of a free workshop on resume building. The strategy would be to think like President Collins and what he did to hire 15 refugees who are supportive to their families today. Dr. Sheila may have friends and relatives who are business owners whom she could talk to and show them that refugees are also human resources.

Those involved in helping refugees or in solving development problems within communities need to learn to attack the roots of the problems rather than the leaves, if they really need to sustainably solve a community problem. From what I have discussed it is good for refugees to have well-built resumes but it is neither enough nor a guarantee for them to have access to job opportunities. My own experience like other many I know is enough. As I said earlier, I have personally helped many people to build their resumes in the past and they were given jobs but I missed a single chance to be hired as soon as I got an employment authorization in the United States.

In San Diego, California accessing (decent) jobs is difficult for asylum seekers as it is for refugees. In fact, it is even more difficult for asylum seekers than it is for refugees. People seeking asylum in San Diego, California are not allowed to work until they are granted work permit by the United States Citizenship and Immigration Services (USCI). This would be considered as a progress because they don't need to wait until their asylum cases are decided upon by an immigration Judge. Furthermore, the timing in processing a work permit for an Asylee from application to delivery is very long (up to four months). Asylum seekers are not entitled to welfare benefits until the immigration court decides on their cases. This may also take up to 3 years or more. However, restricted benefits can be allocated to asylum seekers who are in an emergency situation such as lack of food and medicine but no emergency shelter is provided to them. They have to find their way in a country where they are new and know no one. They can be given only one (1) month food stamps under restricted benefits and medical insurance but the latter may continue in case of health issues.

On the other hand, the first work permit given to asylum seekers is valid for only one year and their Social Security is only for employment, not for other benefits. The work permit expires after a period of twelve (12) months and the Asylees have to apply for renewal of their work permit, which necessitates an amount of three hundred ninety US dollars ($390). This fee can be waived if an asylum seeker shows proof of lower income through a report from the IRS showing their annual incomes. Unfortunately, this proof can neither be obtained free of charge from the IRS nor in time, which causes delays in applying for work permit renewal. In case a work permit expires, the California ID and/or driver's license expires automatically too. The expiration of work permits negatively affects the whole life of asylum seekers in San Diego, California because not only they are stopped to work if they were already employed but also they cannot drive if they had already acquired a car. The expiration of the work permit looks to be synonymous of the end of living in the US. If they stopped from working when their work permits expired; how do asylum seekers survive, pay food, rent and other basic needs a human being needs to survive if there is no other alternatives available to them upon expiration of the work permit? It seems like nobody cares that these people are also human beings who deserve and have the right to life even though they are not Americans. Asylum seekers applying for their first work permit should be aware of the time it takes for the Unites States Citizenship and Immigration Services (USCIS) to process and deliver a work permit; the administration is very heavy that someone might suffer too long before receiving an employment authorization. However, it is observed that some improvement has occurred in processing work permits for asylum seekers over the last few months. Today, asylum seekers can be given a work permit valid for 24 months (2 years) instead of 12 months (1 year) which was given before. Any asylum seeker in the United States should be thankful for this effort. I guess in this matter regarding work permit. The only remaining concern would be to think about how asylum seeker individuals can continue to live during the processing of their work permit renewal.

I strongly think that the hardships which refugees and asylum seekers go through in San Diego, California are the major reason why there are many cases of mental illnesses, increased homelessness, organized crimes, higher rates of prostitution, drug abuse and addiction etc. I think that these are situations which could be prevented by making access to life easy to everyone living in the United States. This is the only war that the United States has failed to win and may continue to fail if critical decisions are not made to mitigate or eradicate these "social injustices" putting human lives in danger on this territory.

Increasing Rates of Prostitution and Drug Use

Poor pay may force refugees to find other means of survival. Sometimes, women and teenage girls engage in prostitution as a means of earning better pay (coincidentally, men and the teenage boys participate in drug smuggling and increased usage). While prostitution has been in existence in San Diego, it has grown over the past few decades as a result of the accumulation of refugees in the area. However, it is important to note that these refugees engage in such acts as a result of lack of favorable and reliable employment.

Due to lack of employment, many parents are not able to give their children the necessary support they need in a country where they have very limited cash aid and very little to no chance to access employment opportunities. Young girls and boys need help with clothing and a little cash that they can use as their "pocket money". Upon their arrival, the youths are given some assistance from resettlement agencies through a program called Wilson Fish (WF). This program helps refugees only for a short period of less than a year after which they are left alone and look for alternative assistance elsewhere which is also very rare to find.

The Refugee Transitional Maintenance (RTM) is cash assistance provided to eligible Refugees, Asylees and Parolees enrolled in the Wilson/Fish Project. This funding is available only for 8 months after initial arrival into the United States and it is conditional based on meeting requirements in the Wilson Fish Program. RTM levels are equal to Refugee Cash Assistance (RCA) levels set by the state. Wilson-Fish (WF) program is an alternative to traditional state administered refugee resettlement programs for providing assistance (cash and medical) and social services to refugees. The purposes of the Wilson Fish (WF) program are to increase refugee prospects for early employment and self-sufficiency, promote coordination among voluntary resettlement agencies and service providers, and ensure that refugee assistance programs exist in every state where refugees are resettled.

The WF program emphasizes early employment and economic self-sufficiency by integrating cash assistance, case management, and employment services and by incorporating innovative strategies for the provision of cash assistance (Alliance for African Assistance).

According to Founders Code (n.d), the purpose of the Wilson Fish (WF) program is to establish an alternative to the traditional state administered refugee assistance program. This is done through the provision of integrated assistance (cash and medical) and services (employment, case-management, English as a Second Language (ESL) and other social services) to refugees in order to increase early employment and self-sufficiency prospects. In addition, the WF program enables refugee assistance programs to exist in every State where refugees are resettled.

Wilson Fish (WF) grantees include States, voluntary resettlement agencies (local and national), and a private non-profit agency that oversees a local voluntary

31

resettlement agency administer 12 state-wide WF programs in the following States: Alabama, Alaska, Colorado, Idaho, Kentucky, Louisiana, Massachusetts, Nevada, North Dakota, South Dakota, Tennessee and Vermont, plus one county-wide program in San Diego County, California.

In most cases, when the youths who were receiving some cash assistance from WF can no longer receive any assistance, that is to say after the eight (8) month period; they are obliged to find ways of helping themselves because they cannot rely on their poor parents. Parents already have many other challenges including, but not limited to, part-time jobs or lack of jobs, insufficient cash aid, etc. In these cases, the only way of helping themselves is to engage in prostitution activities and some time drug use.

Other than the lack of decent work, refugees may also engage in prostitution activities as a result of dealing with idleness. In most cases, the individuals in the resettlement programs do not have anything to do other than staying in their apartments all day. Consequently, they adopt alcohol and drug abuse as a means of keeping their minds off the current problems. A report by Sowey (2005) indicated that a majority of refugee women in California use drugs and alcohol as a means of dealing with stress, insomnia, nervousness, and pain. Furthermore, the report established that a significant portion of these refugees become hooked on the drugs and impose a burden on the community.

Language Barriers

Another major issue that the refugee has had to deal with in San Diego is the language barrier. This problem prevents the refugees from rebuilding their lives in the United States as they had anticipated. Nunez (2017), a reporter at the Global Citizen established that the ESL (English as Second Language) centers that had been set up in various regions in the United States had become defunct as a result of the tight schedules that the refugees had between jobs and taking care of their families. Therefore, since these ESL classes have not been tailored to address the immediate needs of the refugees, these individuals spend between 15 and 24 months without the necessary reading and writing skills. Consequently, they fail to get promotions at the workplace and remain to earn meager pays that cannot sustain them and their families. Furthermore, refugee children who were previously not attending schools have a hard time to mingle with the native kids. It also becomes tough to place these children in schools. In many cases, these children often abandon the need for education as they cannot find suitable schools that accommodate their needs. Besides, the language barrier has barred refugees in San Diego from accessing proper health care and welfare services as a result of lack of interpreters. For instance, resettled refugees from the Democratic Republic of Congo (DRC) cannot find interpreters and/or translators from their background and hence, they opt to be assisted by those from East Africa (Kenya, Tanzania…). However, the Swahili dialects from these two regions are different which makes that interpretation challenging. Similar cases occur to the refugees from various parts of Asia or the Middle East. Such language barriers make communication and interaction between the refugees and the local service providers hard. While such problems continue to impact the lives of the refugees adversely, the resettlement agencies have lagged behind in tailoring possible solutions.

As we all know, helping refugees restart or rebuild their life is the major reason why refugees are resettled in developed countries. Everyone can imagine what restarting a life can look like in a new country; in a country where someone is a stranger and is confronted to a new language.

In San Diego area, refugees are facing many integration issues which, in most cases, are due to language barriers. In this book, I have used a case study of the refugees from the Democratic Republic of Congo (DRC) who speak Swahili language and have many difficulties accessing welfare and other social services offered to refugees. This is because they can't have access to proper interpretation and/or translation services. For instance, in most time, when a Congolese refugee is sick and visits a medical facility the healthcare provider looks for an interpreter and/or translator to help because the patient does not speak English. The refugee patient is given someone from East Africa (Kenya, Tanzania, etc.) who speaks Swahili. Yet the Swahili spoken in those East African countries (pure Swahili) is very different from the Swahili known as Kingwana spoken in the Democratic Republic of Congo (DRC). There are many companies hiring interpreters/translators but neither these companies nor the service providers know about the Swahili language variations. The few who might have learned about this difference think it is a minor issue because there have been no grievances. Congolese are peaceful people who were confronted with war. They will not tell you how they feel about what you do to them until you are able to enter their hearts and find out. The big issue here is to know how to penetrate their hearts to know what they feel! They consider that service providers are mature people and educated enough to know what is good and bad to do the other. (Pastor Ephraim, Congolese refugee, August 2017).

The fact that refugees from the DR Congo suffer from language barriers in their own language (Swahili) and the language of the country they are resettled in has made my interest to conduct further research concerning the same refugee population group. This does not mean that the refugees from the Democratic Republic of Congo are the only refugees suffering language barriers in San Diego, California and the United States at large. Detailed below are the findings of my research about the language barriers among Congolese refugees speaking Swahili language:

❖ *The Swahili Language*

The Swahili language, commonly referred to as Kiswahili, is an African language spoken in the African Great Lakes Region and various parts of Southern Africa. It was developed by the Bantu speakers and serves as the mother tongue of the Swahili community (Safari, 2012, p.7). Swahili is mostly used in Kenya, Tanzania, Burundi, Rwanda, Uganda, Democratic Republic of Congo, and Mozambique. The Comoros Islands, which are close to this region, speak a Comorian language that is associated with Swahili. In some countries such as Tanzania, Swahili has been imposed as the official language while in the neighboring Kenya, the dialect is considered as a national language with proposals of making it an official language being deliberated (Gaw, 2009, p.2). In the Democratic Republic of Congo (DRC), Swahili is regarded as a national language and it is only spoken in the Eastern part of the country (especially in North Kivu, South Kivu, Maniema (the former Kivu region) and in Southern part (Katanga)). As a result of its full acceptance, Swahili has been considered the second most spoken language after Arabic. By putting considerations to the total number of the population in the mentioned nations, the numbers can be seen as being significantly high. The number of its users is further increased by the scattered numbers of its speakers in the Arab world and the big cities in East Africa. The spread of Swahili in regions away from the Great Lakes

Region has necessitated that the users of the language should be careful about their utterances.

People in other regions of Africa and other continents have developed interests in learning the Swahili language (National African Language Resource Center, n.d, p.3). Several reasons have triggered people to learn the language. Some of these reasons include the usefulness to researchers and explorers who visit the East and Central African region, a window to understand the culture of some of the African tribes, and its ease of learning. Furthermore, people who have already learned the Swahili language have found it to be useful when searching for jobs in the Great Lakes Region and also in international organizations that require the applicants to be versant with a local language. Moreover, transnational organizations that have established branches in the East and Central Africa have found that the Swahili language is useful for market penetration.

❖ *Resettled Congolese in San Diego, United States*
The United States Refugee Admission Program (USRAP) initiated the resettlement of Congolese refugees mostly from refugee camps in Tanzania (Center for Disease Control and Prevention, 2014, p.1), there are other Congolese from other camps in Uganda, Rwanda, Kenya, Zambia etc. Refugees from the Democratic Republic of Congo (DRC) in San Diego face numerous challenges that occur as a result of language barriers. Congolese natives speak the Swahili language. However, their dialect of Swahili is different from that expressed in other regions of Eastern Africa. Furthermore, the largest population of the Congolese refugees is illiterate and is only familiar with the oral Kingwana dialect. Therefore, once they have been resettled in San Diego, they are faced with communication challenges that deny them from accessing social amenities and other vital services. These refugees find it hard to buy their food since they don't speak English. The language that they use to express themselves cannot be understood by the rest of the population. Many of them prefer to buy food products from certain African markets where items are very expensive yet their Food Stamp known also as CalFresh money is just planned for a month and not more. This causes them to go without food around the 20th of the month because they spent a lot in the African market. Furthermore, these individuals have a lot of trouble accessing healthcare services, moving from

one place to another; children are unable to understand anything taught in schools, engaging in community-based initiatives is problematic. They also find themselves breaking the laws of the country unintentionally. The Congolese refugees need to find interpreters and/or translators that will be helpful in ensuring that they can interact with the American population. Interpreters/ translators with knowledge of Swahili may be available in San Diego, but the biggest problem is that they are only knowledgeable about the East African Swahili which is different from that spoken by the Congolese. While some words may be shared between the two Swahili dialects, a majority of them depict different meanings. Therefore, a refugee may be requesting something in their version of Swahili, but the interpreter/translator showcases a different meaning of the same. The unsual part of the 2 Swahili is that many words are opposite or different to the others or just don't exist in the other Swahili. For example: the verb *to buy* in the Swahili (Kingwana) spoken in the DR Congo means *to sell* in the Swahili spoken in East Africa (Kenya and Tanzania). Therefore the Congolese refugees in the United States continue to face significant challenges which make their social lives unbearable as reported by The Guardian (2016, p.1).

From my findings during my research on this issue; it looks like none of the service providers in the United States, particularly in San Diego, know about this problem. It is unfortunate that interpreters/translators from East African countries who are serving in San Diego are very much aware of these language variations but they cannot inform the service providers in order to keep their jobs and continue making money. There is a code of Ethics for interpreters and/or translators and there is no doubt that they know about these discrepancies.

Other refugees speaking other languages such as Arabic from African countries and Asian countries may feel the same frustrations when it comes to Arabic language interpretation and/or translation but this might be of a very low incidence on refugees ability to cope up with the life in San Diego because the differences might be only in the flaw of the language but not in the meanings of the words like French language from Canada and French language from France. Although I did not focus our research on other languages spoken by other refugees in San Diego it does not mean that they are not suffering from language barriers preventing refugees from starting a new life in the United States. Our main focus was on the refugees from the Democratic Republic of

Congo (DRC) who speak Swahili language because we have witnessed how this group of people suffers from language barriers and the consequences are greatly high.

One of the terrible situations which led my research was the case where a Congolese refugee (whose name was kept confidential in this book) was scheduled for an eye surgery at the Eye Surgery Clinic in San Diego. The eye Surgeon himself has experienced the differences between the Swahili which was spoken by the patient and the one spoken by the interpreter hired. The two men (patient and interpreter) could not understand each yet they were both speaking the same language "Swahili". In this case, the interpreter could not inform the doctor about his language limitations but the patient was saying that he was not able of understanding what the interpreter was saying. As it was done over the phone, someone not informed would think it was a network connection problem. Not at all, but it was the language barriers problem. For the rest of the process, the surgeon asked the patient to come with his own interpreter instead of the ones who don't understand the other Swahili dialect spoken by the patient.

Another refugee woman who was in labor at a Sharp Hospital had the same problem as the nurses were preparing her for cesarean. Someone may say that it is not a big issue because these examples are only two (2) but examples are very many even though we cannot list all of them in this book. The healthcare field is a very sensitive one and there should not be any single mistake of this kind. It is about lives of human beings and therefore should be taken seriously. It is in my belief that the patient must understand all that is said by the doctor. Therefore the interpreter/translator must be able to deliver the message accurately and faithfully. This is even very well stated in Interpreter/translator Code of Ethics. Refugees from the Democratic Republic of Congo (DRC) suffer doubly from language barriers. First they don't know English language because French is the official language of their country. The latter is spoken only by those who got a chance to go to school from back home. Secondly, their Swahili language known as Kingwana is very different from the pure Swahili spoken in East African countries where most interpreters hired by service providers come from.

It should be clearly understood by readers that I have nothing negative against my fellow interpreters and/or translators from East African countries (Kenya and Tanzania). These countries, in fact, are friends of the Democratic Republic of Congo (DRC) and their citizens are friends to the Congolese. My only point is to raise awareness about this problem putting Congolese refugees and other refugees at risk of death in San Diego, California. In this book, I talked about other issues related to the multifaceted problems of management of refugee resettlement in the United States but I deployed more efforts on language barriers. I will speak more and more about this problem at all occasions and that will be my contribution to stop what is already and may continue to be disastrous if nothing is done immediately. In fact, one of the ways to prevent Congolese refugees from facing these problems continuously is to train the existing interpreters/translators in the Swahili (Kingwana) vocabularies. Then they will be able to interpret and/or translate for those refugees without causing troubles. The training would consider the conception, production and publication of a Kingwana handbook as a reference for interpreters and translators.

My book does not attack either the companies hiring Swahili interpreters and/or translators. I want them to continue to be very successful in their business while striving to save human beings' lives. It would be also very much appreciated if they could be supportive to this initiative by following my suggestions to tackle these problems. Doing more research about the languages in which they offer interpretations and translations is also paramount.

I have talked a lot about language barriers among Swahili speakers from the Democratic Republic of Congo (DRC) and, as I mentioned, many other refugees are going through the same problems although I had no chance to focus on more than 1 group of refugees.

Now allow me to walk you through the challenges associated with Language Barriers among Swahili speakers from the Congolese Refugees in San Diego, United States of America:

- ***Language barriers and Access to Quality Healthcare Services***
The situation in the Democratic Republic of Congo (DRC) has brought the rise of diseases that have claimed the lives of millions of civilians. Those refugees

who succeed in acquiring visas and being resettled in the United States are thoroughly scanned for any diseases that pose threats to the American community (Division of Global Migration and Quarantine, 2016, p.3). However, when these refugees are resettled in areas such as the City Heights, San Diego, the risk of diseases outbreaks emerge as a result of the overcrowding. After falling ill, the refugees seek medical attention from the local healthcare centers. The majority of native Congolese is only well-versed in their local language, Swahili (Kingwana). Those who have knowledge of French are few and in many cases fail to be well-versed with the language. Therefore, the Swahili speaking Congolese require interpreters and/or translators who will help them express their signs and symptoms to the physicians.

In cases where the interpreters/translators are unavailable, it becomes complicated to treat the patient. The healthcare practitioners are, in most cases, not conversant with the Swahili dialect and therefore, the Congolese patients are barred from receiving quality medical care. In such instances, the doctor is forced to either to send the patient back home or to guess prescriptions which pose a threat of death to the patient. On the other hand, the physicians may be forced to turn down the refugee's request of administering medication which is also equally dangerous to the patients (Espinoza, 2016, p.1). In instances where an East African interpreter/translator is present, it becomes a bit easier for the doctor to prescribe medication to the patient. However, the disparities in the meanings of words may also result in confusion which is equally precarious to the patient. It should be mentioned that numbers and days of the week are said differently in the Swahili spoken by East African interpreters/translators and the Swahili (Kingwana) spoken by Congolese refugees. We all know how the use of numbers and the days of the week can be very important in medicine prescriptions. For instance, one must know when (date and day) the pain started and when (day and time) to take medicine after the doctor's appointment. Therefore, the language barrier problem facing refugees from various regions who settle in the United States has left them prone to poor access to medical services as well as death due to misdiagnosis (Morris et al., 2009, p.534).

- ***Language barriers and Education***

Every resettled refugee has a right to all necessities including education for the children and youths. However, in cases where the refugees are not well-versed with the English language, it becomes hard to concentrate in class. As a consequence of the latter, the resettlement agencies, in collaboration with the federal and state governments, have set up English as Second Language (ESL) centers that help in ensuring that the refugees are enlightened on the use of the English language (Endicott, 2016, p.1). However, as reported by Garett (2006, p.7), many of these ESL centers have been mismanaged which leaves a significant proportion of the refugees unaware of how to communicate in English. The Congolese refugees also have a hard time in schools because they are not versant with the English language. This creates a need for inter-preters/translators to be provided at some points in ESL classes.

However, the fact that a majority of these interpreters/translators speak the East African Swahili places them at a disadvantage. Therefore, the latter leaves a majority of the children feeling out of place and they can eventually drop out of school or reduce their interest in education because of the lack of proper communication. While a small proportion of the Americans have shown in-terest in learning Swahili, they mainly study the dialect spoken in the East African nations such as Tanzania and Kenya rather than the Congolese Swahili (Kingwana) which is more uncommon. Therefore, this places the Congolese refugee children in a position that they cannot access quality education despite resettling in United States.

- *Language barriers and the Access to Employment*
Resettlement agencies are required to provide the refugees with start-off jobs in companies found in the areas where they are relocated. However, in many cases, these jobs are demeaning and unworthy despite the problems facing the refugees. Therefore, many refugees tend to quit from these posts and search for more promising ones. Furthermore, some of these refugees may be well-educated and find that these casual jobs to be way below their pay grade. Another major challenge that Taylor et al. (2016, p.7451) suggested is that they flood the local economy which brings stiffer competition between them and the natives. When the Congolese refugees go in search of employ-ment, the fact that they rely on Swahili makes it difficult to communicate with the firm owners. Therefore, they are forced to work as casual laborers where they can only earn minimum wage. However, some companies in San Diego and other regions of the United States have been known to take ad-

vantage of the refugees and give those wages that are below the agreed minimum. Additionally, when these refugees are in the workplaces, their counterparts who are American natives, may develop a tendency of ill-talking about them when they are still present in the room (Human Rights Watch, 2001, p.1). They may even go to the extent of scolding them just because they cannot understand the English language. Such cases have a negative impact on the overall performance of the refugee who feels less appreciated and demeaned despite working hard.

- *Language barriers and Constant Conflicts with the Law*

Many of the Congolese refugees cannot read the American constitution because it is written in English and there are no Swahili translations for the same. Therefore, these individuals may break the law unknowingly. They end up facing the same repercussions as those who know English language. Furthermore, the Swahili interpreters/translators are scarce and hence, they do not offer much help to the Congolese refugees. For instance, one or two Swahili interpreters may be found in an entire region such as in the City Heights where the largest population of the refugees is resettled in San Diego. Therefore, these refugees are forced to travel far and wide in search of people who are familiar with their language and may help them to synthesize some of the basic laws of the United States. The same problem of conflicting with the law has also affected other refugees from regions such as Syria, Palestine, and Jordan (Prettitore, 2016, p.1). Most of the refugees from other countries living in San Diego and other parts of California are organized into communities and they help one another, which is a different case for refugees from the Democratic Republic of Congo (DRC). They are not organized as a community due to their country background characterized by war conflicts, ethnic differences and lack of support.

Congolese refugees who came to San Diego over the last 15-20 years have said they have tried several times to get organized as a community in order to help one another but they have always been discouraged due lack of support. Many other refugee groups are organized in communities and supported. That helps them to be also supportive to individuals from their countries. Being organized into a community could be helpful to Congolese refugees in many ways.

- *Language barriers and Transport Issues*

One significant difference that can be observed between the United States and the DR Congo regards the infrastructural development. Furthermore, while many people live in urban settings in the U.S, the largest proportion of individuals in the DRC live in the rural areas. As such, when the Congolese refugees are re-settled in areas such as San Diego, they have a difficult time moving from place to place in and out of the city. All road signs are written in English which makes comprehension by the Congolese refugees impossible because they only know how to read in Swahili (Kingwana) and some French (only those who are educated). Research by Segal and Mayadas (2005, p.566) suggested that the issue of transport has been a major drawback to refugees accessing social services such as healthcare and stable jobs.

The refugees are also unaware of the meaning of various road illustrations. Apart from reading the signs, the Swahili speakers cannot lease a vehicle because of the lack of comprehension of the English language. Therefore, they fail to establish a conversation with the leasing personnel. The use of cabs is also another major issue among the Swahili-speaking Congolese refugees because many drivers are not versant with the Swahili language. As reported by Bose (2011, p.20), the refugees are unable to communicate with the drivers regarding where they are going or where to alight. The above situation also limits the movement of the Congolese speakers, and they are left to search for alternative means of transport. Public transport is the only choice left which is also not much comfort for the Congolese refugees in San Diego. The same case as to that in cabs happens in public transport whereby the refugees are unable to communicate with the coach drivers. Furthermore, they remain unaware of where the bus stops are situated and in many cases; they find themselves in the wrong destinations. I think this situation will continue to cause them more worries about their life in the country if nothing is done to mitigate language barriers.

- *Language barriers and Making Purchases*

Retail stores, convenient stores, and other shopping outlets in San Diego and across the United States have many customer aides who are often English speakers. However, in some cases, some stores have French, Spanish, and other language speakers as their aides. Therefore, refugees who are not versant with these languages face serious problems during making purchases as suggested by Nunez (2014, p.1). Nonetheless, it is tough to find a convenient store with Swahili-speaking aides in San Diego. The few who are present in these stores are East African natives who, as seen in earlier discussions, speak a different Swahili from the Congolese. As a consequence, the Congolese refugees have a hard time making purchases in these stores as well as other places. For instance, the Congolese refugees can find it difficult buying groceries because they are labeled in English whereas they only know them by their native language. As a slice of bread is better than no bread at all (Drucker, 2006); Congolese refugees travel long distances in search for an African markets when they can understand a little bit of Swahili from East Africa with all the risks of having their food stamp or CalFresh money consumed in only a couple of purchases. Besides, the interpreters/translators available from East Africa tend to have different names for the greens and cereals which make things for these refugees harder. As a result, the Congolese refugees are forced to conduct blind and impulse buying during their shopping sessions. They may find themselves with items that they never intended to use or spend money on. The latter tends to reflect negatively on their limited resources that are provided by the resettlement agencies, welfare services and other contractors.

- ***Language barriers and Non-inclusion in Community-based Initiatives***
Community projects require the participation of all members of the society regardless of their religion, race, or ethnicity. However, research conducted by West Midlands Strategic Partnership for Asylum and Refugee Support (2009, p.38) found that refugees are often sidelined during community development agendas. The same situation faces the Congolese refugees in the San Diego region who find themselves excluded from communal activities because they cannot coordinate properly with the rest of the members because of the language differences. In other cases, Nawyn et al (2012, p.271) found that these individuals do not see the need to engage in these activities and prefer secluding themselves from the rest of the community because they feel inferior to the natives. Therefore, the Congolese refugees miss out on opportunities that are presented to them and which may be helpful in their daily lives. For instance, during community sports engagements, the Congolese refugees fail to participate because coordinating with other people is problematic.

The same problem of non-inclusion in community-based initiatives may apply for refugees from other parts of the world but it can be mitigated in their respective organized communities. Those from the DR Congo remain permanently victims because of lack of an organized Congolese community which could be able to guide them whenever needed and in whatever is needed.

I must remind my readers that, although I focused on language barriers among Swahili speakers from the Democratic Republic of Congo (DRC), I recognize the existence of other refugees from other parts of the world who are suffering from the same problems. I know very well that many other refugees are going through the aforementioned problems related to language barriers when it comes to accessing public services such as healthcare services, welfare services, and schools. For instance Refugees from Iran and those from Afghanistan speak the same language (Farsi) but there are many variations in the same language among people from those two countries. According to Kelly Wright, Global Village Program Manager at Alliance for African Assistance (September, 2017); there have been many complaints among refugees from those two countries too when it came to interpretation and/or translation services. A refugee from Iran may not understand what an interpreter from Afghanistan says yet they speak the same language (Farsi) and vice versa for a refugee from Afghanistan dealing with a Farsi interpreter/translator from Iran when trying to access public services in San Diego.

Considering the number of countries where Farsi is spoken (Afghanistan, Iran, Iraq, Oman, Qatar, Tajikistan, etc.) and the fact that there are many refugees from these countries in the San Diego, California and other states of the United States of America (USA); there is a possibility to think that a great deal of number of refugees are suffering language barriers which makes it difficult for them to have proper access to public services.

According to Farsinet (n.d); Farsi, also known as Persian Language, is the most widely spoken member of the Iranian branch of the Indo-Iranian languages, a subfamily of the Indo-European languages. It is the language of Iran (formerly Persia) and is also widely spoken in Afghanistan and, in an archaic form, in Tajikistan and the Pamir Mountain region.

Persian is spoken today primarily in Iran and Afghanistan, but was historically a more widely understood language in an area ranging from the Middle East to India. Significant populations of speakers in other Persian Gulf countries (Bahrain, Iraq, Oman, People's Democratic Republic of Yemen, and the United Arab Emirates), as well as large communities in the United States.

Total numbers of speakers is high: over 40 million Farsi speakers (about 60% of Iran's population); over 14 million Dari Persian speakers in Afghanistan (50% of the population according to CIA World FactBook & Britannica); and about 2 million Dari Persian speakers in Pakistan.

There is high need to tackle these language barriers among refugees in order to help them live a stress free life in San Diego, California and the United States of America in general. We have practical and very good strategies to end or at least alleviate these issues if we can be given an opportunity to help. One of the strategies to help in this case would be to make sure there is a good number of trained interpreters/translators in these languages causing problems and mobilize people from the refugee groups affected by the problems to become interpreters/translators. However, I must argue those who hire interpreters/translators that there is a difference between speaking a language and interpreting or translating a language. The fact that a person speaks a language does not mean that he/she can interpret/translate that language. Training first!

Unwelcoming Communities

While many people may seem content with welcoming refugees into the country and in the neighborhoods where these agencies settle them, another portion fails to embrace these individuals. As earlier discussed, some people have painted a bad image about the resettled refugees. Consequently, other individuals are made to believe that these people are what they have been described. For instance, refugees from the Middle East or Muslims are branded terrorists based on their nationality and religion (Garret, 2006). This stereotyping of these individuals is derived from the recent cases of terrorist attacks in Europe. Furthermore, recent radical incidents in Southern California have also led to the rise of fear and unwelcoming attitudes towards the refugees.

The refugees lead a life of fear in their houses as a result of constant threats from their neighbors. In fact, refugees have fear while interacting with other people in the society because of the unwelcoming nature that they may have witnessed in their first days of arrival. Rather than feeling welcome and contented with their new life in the country, the refugees feel intimidated and develop the feeling of rejection which has an impact on their mental state.

Stereotyping refugees in our respective communities is a great mistake because no one at all in this world will ever choose to become a refugee. Many people also tend to ignore the difference or assume there is no difference between a refugee and an immigrant although the two seem to have the same meaning but the difference is important for economic, social and legal reasons. For just a very short reminder; let us look at the differences between refugees and immigrants according to The New Americans (2003):

➢ **Refugees**
   Refugees are forced to leave their home countries because of war, environmental disasters, political persecution and/or religious or ethnic intolerance. They come to the United States with a special immigration status that gives them automatic admission into the country and helps them connect with family members who are already in the country. This status also provides them with a "green card" or a permit to work. Refugees are "invited" by the government to live in the United States to start a new life.

➢ **Immigrants**
   Immigrants generally come to the U.S. for one of two reasons:
   • they are joining family members who already live in this country
   or
   • they are "economic immigrants" seeking work and a better life for themselves and their families

Immigrants and refugees have a good deal in common. They experience new cultures and languages. They are often ethnic minorities who might face open discrimination or other forms of hostility, regardless of their immigration status.

We can learn more about this through to the answers in the question below which was answered in The New Americans (2003):

Why do immigrants and refugees come to Iowa?

Immigrants and refugees live in Iowa for the same reasons other residents live here. Most are drawn by the availability of jobs. Many arrive to take jobs in meat-packing and other agricultural industries. But as time goes by, more newcomers work in other sectors of the economy, including construction, services, retail and hospitality. In many communities their labor is in great demand.

Newcomers also appreciate Iowa's low cost of living, affordable housing and safe communities. Just like established-resident Iowans, immigrants and refugees realize their children receive a fine education in the schools. For refugees and immigrants, living in Iowa provides an opportunity to start a new life for themselves and their children. Iowa provides an opportunity for thousands of newcomers to live their version of the American dream.

I want all of us to understand that the differences given here between refugees and immigrants should not be a reason why we can discriminate or stereotype one or another group in our respective communities.

In opposition to refugee and immigrant life in the State of Iowa, life is still very hard for refugees in San Diego, California where living conditions are very expensive to an extent that people may wonder what is the true reason why refugees are brought or resettled in a luxurious State like California.

From the differences well explained by The New Americans; I think that immigrants may be able to survive in a deluxe state because they get time to prepare themselves to leave their home countries. They make their decisions ahead of time; therefore they may have some resources to help them survive once in the United States. But as we understand, refugees leave their home countries mostly in a very clandestine way; they are forced to leave because of fear of persecution and therefore have no chance to go with necessary things they may need in their second country of refuge. Besides, refugees spend a considerable length of time in refugee settlements or refugee camps (usually

15-20 years) where they are traumatized more by life conditions before they get a chance to be resettled in developed countries.

Stereotyping or discriminating refugees is another form of psychological torture after they have gone through moral and physical torture from their home countries. As members of the community we should encourage others to understand the necessity of a peaceful cohabitation and always strive for a welcoming environment in our respective communities. Let us make it easy for refugees to feel loved and/or welcomed as new members of our communities. Always keeping in mind that no human being can predict the future; a refugee we pigeonhole today can become part of our family tomorrow.

There are many consequences that can result in poor welcoming practices or stereotyping new comers in our communities. We have seen many problems of that kind over the last 2 decades. For instance, in 1994, after the genocide in the republic of Rwanda hundreds of thousands of refugees fled their country to the Democratic Republic of Congo (RDC) which, at that time, was known as Zaire. The United Nations High Commission for Refugees (UNHCR) prepared settlement camps for these refugees to live as they were looking for peaceful place in order to save their lives. At that time I was 18. I saw these refugees suffering a lot with very limited to no chance to find jobs, shelter and live like other Zairian citizens. Those who were from rich families were able to start up some businesses immediately which enabled them to employ other refugees. And those who were poor remained subjected to hard labor jobs working for citizens all days long to be able to feed their families. I saw many people among the citizens who were not happy at all to see refugees come to our land saying that they are eating our food, they are spoiling our environment, they are dirty people, they don't speak our language, they are bad people, many of them are very thin as if they were sick... Our parents could not allow us to play with their children! I really saw them living under almost the same stereotypes that refugees live in other countries where they are not welcomed by community members.

When the so called "liberation" war started in my country, the refugee camps were demolished and many of these refugees dies in the war as they were among the most targeted by the Rwandan army which came to support the rebels to chase President Mobutu who overstayed on power. The refugees who got the chance to escape the killings moved into the neighboring forests and national parks where they got very well organized and eventually received some support in weapons from somewhere. They started coming back into our villages to kill, rape our mothers and sisters including small babies. They were attacking during day time or at night as they wanted because there was no organized force to prevent them from persecuting the local populations. During their actions, we could hear them say openly: "now it is time for you to pay all you did to us when we came to this country as refugees because you were not good to us as if we made ourselves refugees to this county. We will make you pay up to the very last penny," they said.

By talking about this experience of bad memory, I am not saying that refugees who are being resettled in the United States can act like those from Rwanda, and I am not encouraging them to do so, but I am just showing how unwelcoming communities can make refugees feel bad and keep those bad memories. It is time for people to change the ways they look at others no matter which part of the world they come from, no matter the color of their skin, their religious beliefs or any other situation that can lead them to stereotyping those coming to live in their communities. Nobody chooses to become a refugee but people are forced!

In this modern time I am still seeing people in our communities who don't understand the meaning of diversity. In my exchanges with refugees, those from African countries have reported that they have seen some American citizens leaving a bus, a train or changing seats because they have come to seat near them! If this only this is true, it is a very unacceptable behavior that people must change in a community, especially in a "great" country like the United States. It is very important that those who know the history can help those who do not so that they can understand something about the differences in skin colors, countries where people come from etc. If we were really intelligent enough (and I am sure we are) we should all learn more lessons from our Mother Nature. Let us take a few moments to look at the Nature in our environment: look at the flowers, look at the trees, look at the animals, and look at the birds and everything that exists and breaths. What would this beautiful world look like if there was only one kind of everything that we see in the nature? I think diversity makes our world look more beautiful!

Difficulty in Accessing Healthcare Services

After being resettled, refugees have a hard time transitioning and feeling whole again. They suffer from stress, depression, and constant worry that lead to poor health. These issues develop over time since the people are forced to leave their homes up to the time when they are resettled in a developed country. Other health concerns that may affect the refugees include communicable diseases such as Tuberculosis and sanitation-related ailments (for instance cholera). Despite being faced with such health issues, refugees fail to access affordable care from both the public and private facilities. According to research conducted in San Diego by Morris, Popper, Rodwell, Brodine, and Brouwer (2009), a large proportion of the refugees also fail to access healthcare as a result of their beliefs and also the lack of sufficient funds.

Segal and Mayadas further indicated in their research that poor healthcare services delivery could be blamed on the exiting language barriers, family or personal backgrounds, and ethnic issues. Many refugees also hide information regarding their origins and past experiences which can make it hard for the caregivers to prescribe medication. Cultural issues have been known to bring the issue of failure to conform to medical care. In some instances, some of the refugees do not believe in western medication, and hence, they fail to seek medical attention even during critical times. Caregivers who are dispatched to look into the health and living conditions of the refugees also play a part in the poor service delivery. The latter can be explained by the fact that the caregivers fail to be persuasive in need for medical attention to the refugees. Good healthcare should go together with psychological preparation of refugee patients. Preparing them psychologically would be a great deal to help them understand that they can trust the caregivers considering the higher technology, knowledge and health facilities available to them which are very different from those in their home countries and their second countries of refuge.

Two years ago, as I was volunteering to help refugees in the community in San Diego, I received a call from an organization which was working with expecting mothers. They asked me to go and help interpret for a group of refugee women who were receiving help from this organization in their journey to the maternity. Before I joined the group, these women were already going through mental illnesses accompanied by great fear of what maternity would look like in the United States. They had hundreds of questions they wanted to ask in order to know more about the maternity systems in the country. It looked like they had false information which caused them to develop bad feelings about maternity system in the US. Due to language barriers they feared for long time to disclose their concerns and questions to their supporters. The organization really had very experienced women who were also devoted to helping their new friends – the refugee women – and they offered the necessary support an expecting mother would need. They also prepared packages of baby clothing and other items to give to every expecting woman. Unfortunately, despite their desire to assist the refugee women in their maternity journey; they had never been able to stimulate the refugee pregnant women to be open to them so as to discuss their concerns about the American maternity experience.

With the skills I had in Mental Health Interpretation and my certification in Mental Health First Aid, I figured out the needs the pregnant women had in understanding the American maternity system. In most ethnic culture in the Democratic Republic of Congo (DRC) for example, many women don't go to clinics when they are ready to deliver their babies. They deliver their babies from home despite all possible consequences associated with that. Many of those who deliver from their home do it for different reasons which include, but are not limited to, lack of money to pay in the clinic, lack of medical facilities in the areas where they live, long distance between their homes and the clinics, others again believe that using some herbs from home is more helpful to ease childbirth during labor.

When these expecting mothers were getting ready to move to the United States, some of them listened to rumors saying that in the USA the doctors don't give mothers a change to deliver their babies but they rush to proceed with section. African women know that delivering a baby is very painful but it has some other advantages. For instance pushing the baby during labor helps the nerves to be awake and start producing milk for the new baby. African mothers like breast feeding their babies, which I think is really a good practice because it also has many health benefits for the baby as recommend the United Nations Children's Fund (UNICEF) and the United Nations World Health Organization (UNWHO).

My presence in the sessions between expecting mothers and the nonprofit organization which was assisting was very beneficial to these women as they were able to ask questions and receive answers from their fellow women who were teaching them. They were able to disclose all the false information they got before coming to the United States. One of them confessed that she was no longer able to eat, drink, sleep or stand up for a long time because she was already seeing nothing but death at her time of delivery. She had lots of worries which made her develop serious mental health problems as she was approaching her ninth month of pregnancy. Every time she received mail from her provider inviting her for medical appointment, it was a nightmare for her. She eventually missed many of her medical appointments because of the same fears she had already developed. From the day we helped her understand the American maternity system and told her that no doctor will force her to caesarian section; she started smiling again and she confessed that she felt as if she had resurrected from death! On our next session, she testified that she was then able to eat, drink, sleep…and do whatever activities she was no longer able to do not because her pregnancy was big but because she was only seeing death at the time of delivery. A month later, this woman delivered a beautiful baby girl! From this experience, I understood how important it can be to offer psychological preparation to expecting mothers so that they can access healthcare services. I can imagine that there are many refugee expecting mothers who are currently in the same situation but they have no chance to access the counseling services to help them understand the US maternity system.

As we can see, the case described above is about healthcare for maternity. There are other cases in other areas of healthcare services where refugees go through problems and sometimes think that it would be better for them to go back to Africa for treatment. Although there are very limited to no healthcare facilities in Africa; they think they would be treated well or find other means to relieve their pains such as seeking help from traditional doctors who use herbs. About five (5) months ago another refugee whose wife was very sick since they came to the states said his wife visited almost all hospitals in San Diego but she hasn't been able to find the right treatment she needed. He was in the process to ask the provider at a big emergency hospital in downtown to give them a letter saying that they failed to treat his wife and they allowed him to take her to Africa for treatment. When they lived in the refugee settlement in Tanzania in East Africa, they did not have access to quality medicines and well trained medical doctors but every time he could take his wife to the clinic she was able to sleep at least for some days before the situation could change again after a week, two weeks. But in the US she had failed to close her eyes even once in the last 8 months. She has been going to doctors' appointments and emergency rooms. I approached this family again and I showed them that there is no way a sickness that is impossible to be treated in the United States can find cure in an African hospital. The man confirmed that he was serious with his decision to take his wife back to Africa for treatment at least at a traditional or local doctor who will use herbs to help his wife find relief rather than letting her die here in the US. The doctor, with the pressure of the man who was driven by a great emotion to see his wife dying, wrote a letter allowing the refugee man to take his wife for treatment in Africa.

At this point, the doctor missed an opportunity again. This was the time when the doctor was supposed to take a few moments to talk to the refugee man and show him that it is impossible to find a solution in Africa if it is not found in a developed country like the United States – the number one world power. Even if it was not true, the doctor was supposed to tell the refugee man at least one word: "we will fight for you and all will be well my friend" this would have helped the man to keep his emotions from going high and gain courage, trust and maybe encourage his dying wife. As his family was resettled through Catholic Charities, the man took his letter to the resettlement office to explain to them what had happened. As soon as I knew that he got a letter from the doctor allowing him to send his wife to Africa for treatment, I informed the resettlement agency so that they can also help discourage him to send his wife back to Africa. The refugee man had already talked with his wife's relatives in Africa who also accepted the proposition. The funny part of it was that he was not ready to go back to Africa with his wife, maybe because he feared the cost of the air ticket...

On the other hand, many refugees complained that most caregivers take long time to give medication but instead they spend time in tests or examinations while the refugee in serious pain does not find the relief they need. In most cases, the discouragement this situation brings causes them to dodge many medical appointments because they feel like it is just a waste of time.

Lack of clear or good communication can cause many issues in service delivery to refugees especially in the medical field where this can even lead to death. I know that in the United States a patient in much pain goes directly to Urgent Care or to an Emergency Room. Unfortunately, many refugees don't know about this and no one explains them how this process works. They keep thinking that after meeting with their medical provider they will be given medicines before they get out of the provider's office!

Recently, I met another refugee woman who went through surgery in Africa. But because it was not done successfully, she continued to feel a lot of pain even after her family was resettled in the United States. Her healthcare provider planned corrective surgery for her to have some relief, but despite the pain she was going through she said she was not interested in having an operation done in the US because she did not trust American doctors. When I was called again to help with interpretation, we learned that upon their arrival in San Diego they were resettled in an area where residents were looking at them with a "bad eye" which made her feel that their neighbors where not happy to see them in "their country". The stereotype she experienced led her to believe that she will die immediately in the operating room if she accepts to go through a corrective surgery. Yet that was scheduled by the doctor to repair the one she went through in Africa. It really took time and energy to explain this woman that a doctor is there to save people's lives but not to kill people. A psychological preparation session or pre-surgery session was needed to convince this patient.

Another difficulty that refugees encounter in accessing healthcare services is transportation. Many refugees have no cars and none of their relatives own cars to be able to help them. The few friends who may be driving use their cars to go to work. All the refugees have access to medical insurance plans and transportation can be taken care of by the insurance company but it looks like many refugees are not aware of the possibility to use their insurance for transportation to and from the doctor's appointments. Refugees who have had a chance to be assigned mentors by New Neighbor Relief – NNR, a nonprofit organization helping refugees start a new life in the US, ask their mentors to help them with rides to and from their medical appointments. In most cases some of these mentors are only driven by the desire to help refugees navigate in the new culture they don't know that the medical insurance granted to refugees can take care of transportation to and from the hospital. The few mentors who know about this try to call the clinics or hospitals but they deny them the right to speak on behalf of their refugee friends they mentor yet the refugees have language problems which do not allow them to communicate with the provider. In most cases interpretation is either not available at the moment they call or it is very poor and both patient and interpreter don't understand one another.

Hynes (2003) reports that many people in a host nation develop mistrust about the refugees settling in the country. On the other hand, the refugees also have the ideology that they may not be wanted in the country. In San Diego, the refugees have been secluded in particular places which leave them believing that they are unwanted in the area. Other residents know very well the areas where refugees from one or another country are concentrated; therefore they barely visit these areas where there are scores of refugees. For instance, residents know the specific areas where refugees from Iraq, Syria, the Democratic Republic of Congo (DRC) and other African countries, Afghanistan, Korea ... live.

According to Hynes (2003), the refugees develop a sense of being unwelcome as a result of being secluded from the rest of the society. Many people develop a negative attitude towards the refugees by basing their claims on the fact that as soon as their native lands become peaceful, these individuals should leave the country and stop derailing economic prosperity in the host nation.

Problems Accessing Decent Education

When conflicts hit countries, people flee and leave behind their investments and other essential belongings. As for the youth and the teenagers, they are forced to abandon schooling (for those who were enrolled in school). The indication that more than half of all the refugees are children is a confirmation that a significant portion of school-going children are miss out in accessing formal education. When the refugees are resettled in San Diego, California, they find it problematic to find cheap and affordable private schools where they can enroll. They have no other options than to enroll in public schools where they also face many problems starting from adapting to English programs. Furthermore, the differences in the curriculum also pile up to the existing problems. The latter means that it becomes hard to start a new school system that is different from what the individual had been experiencing.

The influx of students in the local schools has been a challenge in San Diego. This predicament arises as a result of the government feeling that it is a burden to facilitate the full education costs of the new students from other nations. A report by the UNHCR (2016) further suggests that while governments may be willing to put up the additional costs, the schools may be faced with a shortage of teaching staff which the administration may be unable to add due to the additional costs involved. Furthermore, teachers in schools with a large number of refugees may find it difficult adapting to the ways of teaching that these children had assimilated in their home nations.

Many refugee children have had their age inaccurately recorded by humanitarian organizations back in the refugee camps. When they came to the United States they were denied school enrollment because of the age written in their records. That is the same reason why we find that all most all the refugees have the same month and day of birth (01/01), they cannot celebrate birthdays because they don't know their exact birth dates! A refugee child of only 15 finds himself/herself with an age record showing he/she is 19, 20 or sometimes 21 years old; yet in American education system a person of that age cannot be enrolled in high school. These refugee children who face this problem are very disappointed. They remain very worried about their life in the country. Many of them end up in streets and find themselves abusing drugs. They may later engage in prostitution activities because they have no other alternatives. All these children who miss the chance to go to school can be a retardment bomb for the whole country.

A very touching story is that of a boy, who was denied school enrollment due to his inaccurately recorded age. At only 16, he badly wanted to go to high school. When a mentor from New Neighbor Relief – NNR, a nonprofit organization helping refugees start a new life in San Diego, California, took him with his sisters for enrollment at El Cajon Valley High School, his sisters were enrolled but he was denied enrollment because it was recorded on his paper work that he was 20 years old instead of 16. The boy went back home crying and very disappointed. He worried about missing the great opportunity to go back to school to prepare for his future! That night he could not eat food and started suffering sleepless nights for many weeks. His parents felt very bad about this but they had nothing to do to help their son enroll in school!

Some weeks later, NNR volunteers came with donations of bicycles to the refugee adults and children in the area. The boy who was denied school enrollment was given a very nice bicycle. He was very happy and smiling. Mentors said they have never seen him in such a mode since he was denied school enrollment. Personally, I was wondering why he was so happy for just a bicycle; said one of the volunteer mentors. The statement made by NNR volunteer created curiosity to know more why and how a bicycle donation changed this boy's life? When I got the information I did my best to approach this boy, he told me that he had a plan with the bike. The plan was to use his bicycle to move around searching for a job that could make him busy as all his brothers and sisters were going to school. He was bored alone at home all day long. Because he was attending a church, he could not join his friends who were wandering in the area engaging in drugs and prostitution. A few days later, he got a job as dish washer in a restaurant in the city of Del Mar at about 30 miles away from East Bradley in El Cajon where he lived. For the last 5 months, this boy has been using his bike to go to and from his job in Del Mar. He has been very supportive to his family which has had a lot of financial hardship, like other refugees, especially his mother who has been ill over the past 9 months (since they came to the US). A month ago, he was involved in a road accident, he was knocked by a car on his way to work but he was not seriously injured apart from little scratches which healed after some days.

This situation is very serious especially for the children whose lives are being disoriented. This causes children to miss the opportunity to prepare their future despite the desire of pursuing their education which burns in their hearts upon their arrival to the United States. Do the government institutions in charge of refugee matters know about these issues and have failed to fix them? Or is this something they are not aware of? I am not very sure about this but I am hundred percent sure that the resettlement agencies working with the government in resettling refugees in the country are very much aware of this problem concerning inaccurate record of refugee children's age. What does it cost to help these children by correcting the age of those whose ages were falsely recorded from the refugee camps when they arrive here? This could help them to enroll in school and prepare their future because education is the key of life and it is even one of the basic human rights. Talking about human rights, when refugee children are denied school enrollment due to their ages which were inaccurately recorded in the refugee camps; they have no other options than enrolling in informal education and/or searching for jobs.

I know, just like any other person does, that these children are given hard labor jobs despite their ages because they obviously cannot be given office jobs. *This means to me that the United States is inadvertently involved in child labor which is a terrible violation of children's rights.*

As I mentioned earlier, it is because of this problem of misrecorded age that about 90% of the refugees, all adults and children, have the same date of birth (mostly 01/01). This information can be verified from the service providers in the country such as the Department of Motor Vehicles (DMV), welfare services, Social Security Administration, immigration services etc. from the identification documents of the refugees!

I have heard about international organizations reports about child labor, violation of children's rights when children were reported to live in streets, to be forced to do hard labor in the mining areas in African countries like the Democratic Republic of Congo. I have seen that the same situation is happening in the United States though not in the mining areas. In many business companies in the United States employees can work up to many hours without seating down, which is something children cannot do.

I think the United Nations Children Fund (UNICEF), Human Rights Watch and other human rights organization who record violations of children rights around the world should record this problem as one of the horrible cases of children's rights violation in the United States. It is unacceptable that children can be subjected to hard labor jobs in a developed country instead of enrolling in school to prepare for their future. In this case, children are forced to street life, they are forced to prostitution, they force to hard labor, they are forced to drug abuse, they are forced to developing mental illnesses when they are denied school enrollment due to misrecorded age. These children going

through these situations are innocent people! They are just victims of what
they don't know. We don't know exactly what this situation makes these children feel and how they can react to this in the future, even 20-30 years after.

According to me this is another situation which should not happen in a country
like the United States. Like many other problems I talked about in this book;
I believe this problem calls for immediate action from those who make decisions in this country as it may continue to tarnish the image of the country if
nothing is done to deal with it.

There are many solutions that I can suggest in order to solve this children's
age miscalculation. One of the solutions I can suggest about this issue is simply
to ask parents what is the exact age of their children immediately as they are
resettled in the county and ignore the age recorded in their travel documents
because it is already known that it is a wrong age (in most cases). On the other
hand, resettlement agencies can work with the United Nations High Commission for Refugees (UNCR) and the United Nations Children Fund
(UNICEF) to fix this children's age problem from their second countries of
refugee before they resettle them in the United States.

As far as lack of descent education is concerned, there are also many suggestions I can make to solve the problem. The most accurate way to solve this
problem, according to me, is to make sure language problem is solved because
it is the root of most of the problems refugee children go through in their education process. If there was no other bad intention (and I'm sure there wasn't)
officers in refugee settlements misrecorded refugees' age because of language
barriers.

Just like the parents are required to learn English as a Second Language (ESL),
resettled refugee children who came from non-English speaking countries
should be given at least 1-2 years learning English language *only* before they
can start normal schooling. Of course, I know that the traditional ESL has
shown it is limitations and needs to be fixed like many reports have shown already. I believe that well structured, well organized and supported Ethnic
Community Based Organizations (ECBOs) can also play a major role in fixing
this problem if they are given a chance. Going from the known to the unknown

could be a great teaching maxim to help refugee children learn English language before they can enroll in normal school program.

If teaching English as a Second Language (ESL) cannot be done through Ethnic Community Based Organizations (ECBOs); it is very important to find other ways to use teachers who speak the same primary languages of the children to be able to teach them English language.

As a teacher, with my knowledge in teaching methodologies, I think this case needs to use the first one from the 12 best maxims of teaching. That is to say *teaching from known to unknown*. Maxims of Teaching are the universally facts found out by the teacher on the basis of experience. They are of universal significance and are trustworthy. The knowledge of different maxims helps the teacher to proceed systematically. It also helps to find out his way of teaching, especially at the early stages of teaching (Notes Read, August, 2015).

Refugee children know already many things in their local languages, their mother tongues. This should be the basis, the foundation to help them step at the gateway to English skills by using the known to unknown maxim of teaching. This maxim is based on the assumption that the student knows something. At this point we are to increase the student's knowledge and widen his outlook. There is need to interpret all new knowledge in terms of the old. It is said that old knowledge serves as a hook on which the new one can be hung. Known is trustworthy and unknown cannot be trusted. So while teaching we should proceed from the known and go towards the unknown. For instance, while teaching any lesson, the teacher can link the previous experiences of the child with the new lesson that is to be taught.

When a child enters into school, he possesses some knowledge and it is the duty of the teacher to enlarge his previous knowledge. If we link new knowledge with the old knowledge our teaching becomes more clear and definite. This maxim (teaching from known to unknown) facilitates the learning process and economizes the efforts of the teacher and the taught. For example in teaching English to the children and the teacher is to teach the word 'water'. He reminds them the Kashimiri word 'Aab' which they already know and then tells them that in English was say 'water'. This way of teaching helps the learners to understand things fully. This way the teaching becomes definite, clearer and more fruitful (Tet Success Key, n.d).

Now if we compare the recommendation of teaching from know to unknown with what is taught to refugee children (and even adults) in learning English as a Second Language (ESL) we can easily realize why it takes refugee learners forever to acquire English skills. Those teaching them know only English and have no knowledge about the refugee primary languages, yet they should be able to go from what the students know to teach them what they don't know. In the example by Tet Success Key, we saw that the teacher went from how students call water in their local language and that helped them to know and keep it in English language. This means that the teacher knew both Kashimiri language and English language. This is exactly what is missing for refugee learners in the United States. I am pretty much sure that my fellow teachers understand what I mean here. It makes me feel so bad when I see that people know the right thing but they continue supporting the wrong one. I am not so sure we can make positive change in our community with such deeds.

I am still very convinced that organized and supported Ethnic Community Based Organizations (ECBOs) can be a good reference to tackle this problem if they are given a chance to contribute. In these organizations we found ethnic leaders and other community members who are educated and who know some English who can help their children and fellow refugee learn the language better than by anyone else. It is only a matter of training them on how to teach English language, give them materials or teaching aids and pay them so that they can make it a job. In fact, it can also create more jobs to the hundreds of unemployed refugees whose education levels are not recognized by employers in the county. Refugee children need 1 or 2 years or at least 6 months of English lessons before enrolling them into formal education programs. And these lessons should be conducted by people who speak the same languages (mother tongues) like them.

Cultural Integration Issues

Refugees originate from all walks of life in different regions of the world. Therefore, these people have varying socio-cultural backgrounds. These backgrounds may fail to integrate well with those of the citizens of the host country (Altshuler, Scott, & Carevya, 2011). For instance, some activities or actions may be common among the Americans, but to the Africans and Arabs, they remain a taboo. Aspects of clothing are one of the main points of concern that bring out the disparity between the refugees and the nationals. Another issue is the food available. It is common to find junk foods being highly appreciated by the Americans, but in areas of Africa, they are firm believers in consuming healthy foods that may be hard to find in the United States. In different get together activities where refugees and volunteers meet on the initiative of New Neighbor Relief – NNR, for example, refugees tend to be distant to American foods which are provided as in cultural integration. Most Americans feel that food tastes better with the amount of sugar in it, whereas Africans feel that salt makes it taste better. Talking about food is cultural integration issue for the refugees. I have also realized that most of the time the food stamps given to them do not last till the end of the month for two reasons: 1. The money for food stamps is never enough and is restricted for some specific items. 2. They spend more money from their EBT cards buying African foods which they like more than American foods. Also, at a certain age a decent African or Arab woman cannot wear pants or shorts when she wants to attend a certain function contrary to an American woman who finds it okay to wear anything she wants whether pants or shorts.

When working with the resettled refugees, service providers have to take into consideration the culture of the people as well as their experiences during the resettlement session. However, the responsible resettlement agencies do not take the time to establish such requirements, and instead, they hope that the refugees will adjust and conform to the way of life of the nationals. There exists a large difference especially between the socio-cultural perspectives of developed and third world nations which make the refugees rigid during the assimilation session (Altshuler et al., 2011). Therefore, with such rigidity, it becomes hard to ensure that the refugees conform to the laid out rules and regulations. Some of their beliefs may also contradict the existing federal or state laws which make them end up on the wrong side of the law unintentionally. In Africa, for example, a man can slap his wife and life will continue very well after, while in the United States it is a big issue which falls under Domestic Violence (DV) of which many refugees are victims or involved every day.

Refugee parents find it difficult raising their children under a new and unaccustomed culture. In many instances, the parents complain that their children become Americanized and forget about their culture which they are meant to follow. Furthermore, kids often catch up in learning English at a faster rate and adapt quickly to the new culture than their parents. Such instances have continued to build a gap between the children and their parents. The different cultures tend to tear these families apart to the point that the parents may disown their children. When families repudiate these kids, they end up on the streets hence piling up to the existing problem of homelessness in the streets of San Diego. Eventually, these children may turn into a life of crime.

I think that well structured, well organized and supported Ethnic Community Based Organizations (ECBOs) can help in becoming culture orientation references for all refugee groups resettled in the United States. These organizations' leaders are supposed to be people who know their own cultures and have long navigated in the U.S. culture. That gives them the necessary knowledge they may need to know about culture differences between the countries where refugees come from and this country in which they are resettled and be able to guide them.

Lack of Personal Necessities

The lack of personal essentials such as clothing and access to clean and safe food and water is a liability to refugees in San Diego. Additionally, personal effects such as toothpaste, bathing soap, and sanitary towels have also been a major concern for these people. This predicament has been brought by the increased rate of unemployment and insufficiency of cash aids. The small amounts of funds they receive from the government and the resettlement agencies are used in paying rent and other utility bills, which amounts never able to help the refugees cover their monthly expenses. Furthermore, the amount given is not sufficient to afford the refugees an excellent meal as well as other personal effects. They have to count very carefully when making purchases to make sure they don't overspend so that their Food Stamps can go up to the end of the month, which is never possible. It should be noted that the food stamps also known in Calfornia as CalFresh do not allow refugees to buy all types of foods they may need or buy hygiene items such as soaps, laundry detergent among others. Children and women are the most affected lot since men can find casual employment that they use to supplement the aids given. When matters spill out of hand, the refugees are forced to beg on the streets of the city. Such actions paint a bad image for San Diego and the United States at large.

Upon their arrival in the United States, refugees are given household items they need to furnish their new apartments. These items include beds and beddings, chairs and tables, sofas, clothing, kitchen supplies (pans, plates, folks, spoons…), liquid soaps etc.

These items are given to refugees only once in their life and that is as soon as they come to the country. After some months the items given to refugees become defective and some refugees feel shame when people visit them because the household items which can be seen by visitors are in a substandard condition yet the refugee families who have already started suffering the insufficiency of their cash aid are not able to replace them. Some nonprofit organizations assisting refugees in San Diego such as New Neighbor Relief – NNR, Alliance for African Assistance, Catholic Charities among others receive in-kind donations and they help refugees with the items they may need in their apartments but these organizations cannot assist all the needy refugees due to limited resources. NNR has set up a warehouse where refugee families come and pick up everything they may need. This organization makes sure all family members come to the warehouse to select the items they need and these include clothing for adults and children, kitchen items, beds and mattresses, pillows, bed sheets, blankets, Televisions, drawers, shoes, toys, strollers, car seats, etc. The reason why NNR requests all refugee family members to come to the warehouse is because they want every family member to pick what they need and what can fit them for clothing and shoes for example. This system helps to avoid that someone takes items to a refugee family and found them thrown in the dumpster if they don't like them or in case they don't fit them because there may be other needy refugees who may need them in the future.

A big challenge associated to this lack of personal necessities is the fact that refugees don't have choices when the household items given to them at the time of resettlement are defective. They take everything given to them by local people in their neighborhood just because they want to replace their old ones. In this case they end up taking items like beds, couches, chairs and table containing many bugs, bed bugs and cockroaches. They even collect items which are already thrown in dumpsters without knowing that they may contain bugs and/or cockroaches which will cost them a lot of money to treat, yet they don't have enough money to survive! Exterminators or Pest control Companies charge up to fifteen hundred US dollars to treat bed bugs and cockroaches in homes. Considering the hardship in which refugees are already living in the country, it would be like causing a disaster to their families to donate items with bugs, bed bugs and/or cockroaches… Recently, a refugee family was complaining about the infection of their apartment by bugs and cockroaches because of items which were donated to them by some people. The president of NNR, a man of great heart, visited this family and decided to sponsor the disinfection of the apartment. The pest control company which was contracted to do this work had some hard time killing these harmful insects. One of the employees of the pest control company confessed to NNR president that since he started that work he has never seen such an infected apartment. Refugees don't come from their second countries of refugee or from the refugee camps with bugs and cockroaches; their bodies and small bags are well screened before they travel to developed countries, their third countries of refuge.

Before accepting donations, New Neighbor Relief – NNR reminds the donors that refugees are also human beings and donating items which are still in good condition will not only honor the donor but also make the refugees feel loved and considered by community members who donated the items. This is something every organization collecting donations for refugees should do with those donating because many people still need to learn the difference between donating and dumping. I think that true donation is when we give out something we could still use but we give it out when we found that there is a needy brother or a sister out there who would be blessed to receive that item.

On the other hand, we have observed that the efforts deployed by New Neighbor Relief – NNR, mentors and other people of good heart who support refugees are being diminished because most refugees lack even the minimum pocket money that they can use when they need to move from one apartment to another. Because they have no money to pay the moving companies; they end up throwing all their household items which were donated to them by those organizations and other people of good will. For instance, some months ago NNR collected and distributed bunches of closing, shoes, household items, bicycles, bunk beds, beds, mattresses, pillows, blankets etc. It was very sad to see that even some of the bunk beds and beddings distributed in partnership with Sleep in Heavenly Peace (SHP) which refugee families were very happy to receive were also thrown away to the dumpsters when the families were moving to other apartments because they did not have means of transportation. This happened when all the refugee families where evicted from an apartment complex in City Heights around Rex Avenue.

From my findings it was observed that dumping household items by refugees is caused by four (4) major elements:

1. ***Resettlement agencies:*** As we discussed in housing problems, some resettlement agencies are obliged to lie to apartment managers about the number of the people who will be living in an apartment because of the restrictions attached to the housing system in the San Diego. Later when the landlords find out about the number of people living in their apartments in reality; they tend to change things and threaten refugee families to throw them out. Resettlement agencies don't take time to search for low income housing or affordable apartments when they look for housing for newly resettled refugees. They put them in very expensive apartments while knowing how much money refugees receive in Cash Aid every month and they know very well that refugee families will not be able to continue paying rent for such expensive apartments. After a while, the families decide to move to other apartments or houses which look a little bit cheap than the previous ones and when they leave they dump their household items because they can't afford moving companies.

2. ***House evictions:*** These happen normally when refugee families are not able to pay the rent fees and the landlords can no long continue to keep them in their apartments. Or, an apartment complex is said to be inappropriate or not viable by the government services and a moratorium is given to them to leave the apartment complex. In such

circumstances refugees have no other alternatives than leaving the apartments and move to others. As they cannot move with their household items; they throw them in dumpsters yet they still need them where they are going.

3. *Lack of employment:* As the Cash Aid received by refugees from Welfare services is never enough to cover all their expenses, refugees families continue to face moves from one apartment to another because they cannot afford to continue living in expensive apartments rented for them by resettlement agencies upon their arrivals to the United States of America (USA). When they move they have no other options that throwing their household items away because they don't have means of transporting them to their new apartments or homes.

4. *Moving to other states:* Due to hardships making it difficult for many refugees to afford the cost of living in California, many refugee families choose to move to other states where they hope to find ways to rebuild their lives. In this case also the refugee families have to throw all their household items away before they move to other states. Upon their arrival to the new states, refugee families will need other household items. From the contacts I made with those who moved to other states it takes them up to 3 months to find other items to use in their apartments. It can take up to weeks or months to those who are members of a church or another religious movement to find donations of household items.

I think it would be better for resettlement agencies to associate refugee families when they purchase household items for them. Most of the refugees are illiterate but it doesn't mean that they don't know what is good and what is bad for their household. Also they should keep in mind the quote by Gandhi saying that "whatever you do for me without me; you do it against me."

Here is what I would do if I was the manager of any resettlement program: Instead of buy all the items at once, I would suggest that resettlement agencies split the money into 2 or 3 portions and keep it to renew household items as soon as those ones bought upon resettlement become defective. This can work for all refugees who lived in refugee camps.

For example: if a family needs 4 saucepans they receive 2 upon arrival and 2 more can be given to them after 12 months. This can help the renewal of household items when the first ones become defective. This is helpful because many refugees spend up to 24 months without jobs. But all must be done in associating the clients in the process and showing them why such a decision is taken.

In my opinion, donating infected household items should be treated like intentionally infecting someone with a virus; therefore it should be published by the laws of the country.

Transportation Problems

Similar to the language barrier, the problem of transportation affects many aspects of the refugees' lives in San Diego and other parts of the United States. Despite there being the illiterate and well-educated proportion of the refugees, a majority of them lack basic education. Therefore, acquiring a driving license is problematic for them. The latter applies for both the documented and undocumented licenses. For the refugees who are qualified drivers and need a license, but so not comprehend English very well, they must be accompanied by an interpreter/translator to help them through the process.

However, these interpreters/translators are hard to be found given that some refugees speak native dialects. Furthermore, to be granted a driving license, an individual must pass an exam which becomes impossible for the illiterate majority of the refugees. It is very difficult for the refugees who do not understand English language to pass the exam, therefore they neither drive in the country nor buy a car until they get a driver's license which may take forever considering the facts discussed above. Yet, owning and driving a car can help them look for jobs and keep the jobs once they get them because they will be independent as far as transportation is concerned. Another big problem is that the driving exam is done on the computer, which most refugees do not know how to manipulate due to illiteracy. The refugees in conflict with English language have a great challenge to prepare their driving exam because California Department of Motor Vehicles (DMV) does not provide booklets in languages known by refugees; all DMV materials are written in English language.

In some instances where the refugees have a private vehicle, it is shared by several families who make it difficult to commute from one place to another (Nunez, 2014). The situation is worsened by the fact that it will be impossible for different families to use the same car to move to and from work and at the same time pick and drop children in school. Besides, men assume ownership of the cars which leaves the women and children finding an alternative means of transport.

On the other hand, public transportation is not a suitable alternative for the refugees. Many of these individuals are afraid of using public modes of transportation such as trains and commuter buses. Their primary concern is the harassment that they face on many occasions. During my research on the multifaceted management problems of refugee resettlement in this country, some of the refugees I approached disclosed that most of the time when they take public transportation; if they take a seat near a citizen the latter stands up after a while to look for another seat. Others get out at the next stop pretending to have arrived and take the next bus or trolley after a short while. Furthermore, a significant portion of these refugees come from rural regions where there are no road signs. Therefore, it becomes an issue for them to know where to board and alight the buses. On top of that, the issue of language barriers also deters them from asking for directions from the other citizens. The same case of traffic laws applies to those refugees who access a driving license, but they fail to be familiar with the road signs and usage (Nunez, 2014). For instance, in some of their countries of origin, they drive on the left side, but when they come to the United States, they find that vehicles take the right hand of the road. Furthermore, the complexity of the city infrastructure overwhelms these refugees. Pedestrians also encounter similar challenges in reading and interpreting the road signs hence commuting in the city becomes hectic.

Another part of the difficulties in transportation is about going to school. In order to keep their welfare benefits, refugees are required by the government to attend English as a Second Language (ESL) class, job search activity or prove their inability to do one of those or both if someone is sick.

The government provides transportation by giving monthly passes to the refugees who are enrolled in the program called Welfare to Work. However, many refugees have got reduced their benefits because they were not able to attend these activities. This has caused many issues to refugees when their benefits were reduced because they have many challenges and the assistance amounts are very limited. During my research about this problem, I found that at some point the government is responsible for their absences to the ESL classes and the same government punishes them in what they are not responsible for. Here is why I think the government is responsible for refugees' absences to ESL classes: For instance on June 14th, 2017 a refugee received a mail from the county of San Diego in which I could read the following: "As of 06/01/2017 until 06/30/2017, the County has approved your transportation for English as Second Lang. The County will only pay for transportation while you are attending your approved Welfare to Work activity: ENGLISH AS SEC LANG

The County has approved $72.00 One Time based on public transportation rates". What a nice letter and a relief for a refugee who is eager to go to school to learn English language and be able to restart his or her new life!

Unfortunately, the mail comes to the refugees before the money is sent to them and it can take couples of weeks, a month or more before receiving the transportation money which was mentioned in the mail. Saying the government means including the contractors such as the Public Consulting Group (PCG), ResCare and others who partner with the government to deliver Welfare to Work programs.

It is really puzzling to read such stories but they are true stories. It is kind of a contrast to threaten people to reduce their benefits – and indeed reduce them – if they don't attend an activity and they understand how important is that activity for them but at the same time not giving them the promised transportation money to help them attend in the activities. I think something is wrong somewhere. The government may not know about this issue but the people who are doing or causing this are acting on behalf of the government. Is anyone out there among my readers able to tell me how understandable is this?

The above situation reminds me a small but amazing story by one refugee woman I visited with my humanitarian companion Daniel T. Collins, the Board

President of New Neighbor Relief – NNR. During our routine visit to his apartment, a refugee man brought a bunch of mail to us so that we could help him to understand what is written in them. The first confusion he had was how the date was written in English. I explained to him that contrary to French style where they start with the day and the month then follows the year (dd/mm/yy); in English (American) they start with the month and the day then the year comes in last position (mm/dd/yy). Everyone in the apartment including the children started laughing and looking at one another. The wife said in Swahili (Kingwana): "Byabo byote biko kinyume na bya wengine hata namna yabo yaku saidia watu". Brace yourselves to hear the meaning of this sentence, it means: "all they do they do it opposite way, even their ways of helping people are opposite". I also laughed a lot while President Collins remained confused but he thought it was something nice we were laughing about.

He asked me to interpret so that he could understand. As soon as I interpreted the sentence for him I saw some drops of tears ready to come out of his eyes but as a man he tried and held them back. He felt very ashamed because of such a perception that refugees have about America. This was my second time to see him in such a mood due to the realities he was learning from these refugees who were sharing their life experience with him. The first time I saw tears in his eyes – and this time he wasn't able to hold them back – was during another routine visit to another refugee family in City Heights where another refugee from the Democratic Republic of Congo, after sharing her life experience in the United States, said in their language (Swahili): "Hakuna hata raha yakuja Marekani" meaning "There is no happiness at all to come to America". Due to hardship many refugees wish they remained and die from their countries or even in the refugee camps!

From that day, during our visits to refugee families, President Collins stopped *asking refugees if they were happy to be in the United States* because he knew already what their answer would look like. Before such an experience, he knew like many other Americans that refugees were very happy to be in the United States as they came from very poor countries, they spent many years (up to 20) in refugee camps but now that they are in the US they have great support from the government, resettlement agencies and other sponsors. I personally can't deny the existence of support to refugees but I think there is need to rethink strategies in order to deliver quality services to the refugees in San Diego, California and the United States at large. I invite anyone else who wishes to ask refugees if they are happy to be in this country to visit at least one (1) refugee family and listen to their life experience stories from since they came to the states up to now. That would also be another way of helping to raise awareness on the refugee sufferings and the many challenges preventing them from starting their new life in the country.

As for the transportation problem, because that is the topic here, there is a need to fix the problem especially by considering the language barriers and lack of education preventing refugees from acquiring a driver's license to own or rent a car. How can someone who doesn't know how to read and write pass a written test. Moreover a computerized test!

Here is what happens: most of the illiterate refugees who need a driver's license go to the DMV knowing that they will never pass the written test on computer. But because they need to have a driver's license to be able to own and/or drive a car they go and take the test. They decide to do the test several times and accept to fail as many times as possible until they succeed. At this point the success is not because they know or understand what they are doing. It is a lottery that they are doing. This changes the meaning of a driver's written test. After passing their DMV computer lottery, they go for a behind the wheel driving test. This one is another nightmare for the refugees. They already have gone through many problems due to language barriers. The instructor conducting the driving test tells them something to do but they don't understand English language. They end up doing something different and the instructor mentions the mistakes on the long form. At the end of the test, it is concluded that they have failed the behind the wheel driving test! Because they need the driver's license very badly, the refugees will not be tired to take their test. They will continue to do it as a lottery, the same way they did for the written test on computer until the day they will succeed the test. Later on they involve in many road accidents because they acquired driver's license through playing lottery but not that they understood the traffic rules.

My own experience has taught me much of what refugees who want to drive a car in the United States go through. I am a little bit educated and from my country I drove since I was 17. My father owned a very old Volkswagen (VW) and at when I was only 16 my elder brothers were stealing it, took us all in it and went to a football ground near Murhesa parish where everyone was learning to drive. I started renting cars and drive when I was 25. I owned my first car when I was 28 years old. I came to the United States when I was 40. I went to take my driver's test at the DMV when I got my work permit and Social Security cards. The written test was not a big issue for me because, not only I knew how to drive a car but also, I knew how to use a computer. I got my driver's permit and started doing more exercises to be familiar with driving in the U.S.

After succeeding this written test; I had to go through the behind the wheel test for my driver's license. When came to the DMV to take my driving test, the instructor started by asking questions before starting the car and I failed to understand what she was saying because I did not know the parts of the car in English. I told her I knew everything in French but not in English. She told me: "my friend this is America and the test is done in English". We went out for driving, she told me what to do at every step and I did what I could understand and left what I didn't understand. After moving around the neighborhood the instructor told me to go back to the DMV office. When we arrived in the compound, she pulled her form and told that I failed the driving test. I started laughing to see that I failed a driving test after driving for over 20 years.

People who were present waiting for their turn to take their driving test remained surprised that I was laughing after failing my driving test. One of those who were waiting asked: "why are you laughing after failing your test? Many people feel very sad when they fail but it looks like you feel happy". I told this man that I was laughing because I was surprised by my failure to drive a car after driving over 20 years in my country and neighboring countries.

I succeeded the test on the second trial.

At that moment I really started wondering what happens to my fellow Africans and others refugees who have no driving experience, no English language skills at all but they still need a driver's license.

Insufficiency of Cash Aid

Refugees rely heavily on the aids from the resettlement agencies, the federal government, non-governmental organizations, and other private donors. The mentioned bodies are responsible for visa preparations and travel costs for the resettled refugees. Upon arrival in San Diego, the resettlement agencies are tasked with the duty of ensuring that these people are given the necessary monetary support they deserve until they have fully settled. The above means that the agencies must source a lot of funds to ensure that these people are well taken care of in the places they settle. It is the expectations of the organizations that these individuals get jobs so that they can help them as they rebuild their lives in the shortest time possible (Spracklin, 2017). However, due to other associated factors, the refugees either get poorly paying jobs or fail to access any employment. Therefore, the agencies are forced to continue giving the necessary monetary support to these families. Over time, this has become a burden to the agencies especially in San Diego where the influx of refugees is high. The number of refugees who depend on these agencies has increased over the years. This means that the agencies can only split the limited resources to a large crowd of people. For this reason, it has turned out to be difficult for these individuals to access essentials such as food, proper housing, and private medical care.

Complaints raised by some members of the Congress have been associated with the small cash aids that refugees receive in all places inclusive of San Diego. These members present their cases that the federal and state governments are wasting a substantial amount of resources by channeling them to refugee aids. They further insist that these funds could be useful in strengthening the economy through making capital investments in infrastructure. Such sentiments have been backed by residents who feel that the refugees are consuming a lot of funds that can be used for other national projects. Therefore, to ensure that such grievances are addressed, the government may be forced to narrow down the resources dedicated towards the resettlement of refugees. Report by the California Department of Social Services (2016) indicated that resettled refugees receive cash aids from the federal, state, and county administration but these figures were decreased in the 2016 fiscal year. Such incidences of reduction in cash subsidies have a direct impact on the living status of the refugees. For instance, these people may be forced to move from their houses because of inability to pay the rent. As a means of solving this problem, many refugees pool their resources and live in the same house and also share other available resources. By so doing, they may end up causing congestion in particular areas which property owners are unwilling to compromise. Furthermore, the threat of insecurity also increases since people are inclined to live with other people whom they were not familiar with under the same roof. Efforts to increase the amount of cash aid given to these refugees have dwindled especially due to the increase in the number of refugees in the region.

Regardless of the fact that the Cash Aid is already insufficient and does not help the refugee families to cover all the monthly expenses for rent, utilities, clothing, hygiene products etc., government services such as welfare services have exceeded in reducing or cutting Cash Aid to refugees families in San Diego. The first victims of this practice are illiterate refugees forming the majority to the refugees from African countries for example. Refugees receive mail on a regular basis and they are obliged to read and understand them (even if they don't know how to read). If they don't reply to some mail such as reporting how they are using their cash aid and other matters, they will have their benefits reduced or cut off completely. The majority of the refugees, from Africa for instance, are illiterate they don't know how to read and write. They receive large amounts of papers to read, fill up and return to welfare offices. This makes another great challenge facing them because they don't know how to fill in these important papers. Some refugees end up thinking that the brains of those working in welfare offices don't function well because they know very well that the refugees are illiterate in English but they keep sending them packages of papers to fill in and return. "I am very flabbergasted by welfare service, I did not go to school but I cannot think like them; how can they give all these papers to someone who does not know how to read and write and ask him/her to fill them up?", said a refugee I interviewed in Lakeside area. He received a package of forty-eight (48) papers of seventy-nine (79) pages and he was asked to fill them and return to welfare office. When I had a look at the package, it was really something voluminous and not easy to understand by someone who has never gone to school. I realized it needed a certain education level (which the refugee didn't have) and considerable time to answer the questions asked.

On the very first page of the package in the package I could read the following:

CalWorks – CW
Renewal-RRR
English
Complete – Sign and Return.

This refugee family was lucky that I passed by their apartment and I was able to help them fill in the papers. My great concern about the amount of papers given to illiterate refugees to "Complete – Sign and Return" remained as I was wondering what would happen to other hundreds of illiterate refugees who receive the same package and have no chance to be visited by literate people who can help them fill up these papers?

On the other hand, during the resettlement process in the second country of refugee, the International Organization of Migration (IOM) gives Travel Loans to refugees. Many of the refugees interviewed said they were very excited for their journey to the United States and they didn't care much or realize how hard it would be to pay back their travel loans. This is another reason why refugee orientation should be well focused and truthful in order to prepare refugees very well before they come to this country. Everyone will accept a loan when they tell them that upon their arrival in the United States they will be given jobs and start reimbursing their travel loans. A part from the travel loans, refugees take other loans from local business people and take their family members or friends who remained in the camps or city where they came from as guarantors of their loans. They know that, as they are told during orientation, upon their arrival in the United States they will be given jobs in order to start getting incomes and be able to pay back their loans. Apart from these loans, all family members who remained in their second country of refugee will start relying on them because they know that dollars are from the U.S. They think their relatives will start harvesting U.S. dollars as soon as they step on U.S. land.

The question most refugees always ask is: "would there be any problem if the resettlement agencies could tell their partners in charge of conducting orientation before the refugees travel to inform the refugees that it is not easy to find jobs as a refugee or it takes long for refugees to get jobs in the United States?" Why not tell refugees the truth about the kind of life awaiting them so that they can come when they are more prepared instead of coming with many expectations which will be destroyed as soon as they arrive here? (Said another refugee who talked to me during my interview on insufficiency of cash aid).

Many refugees said they were never told that they will have to go to school for many months or years before they can start working. Others, however, complain that they were farmers they never went to school, they are illiterates and those who resettled them knew about their background before bringing them but by surprise they were brought to a state like California (in concrete) where life is very expensive and where they cannot practice their farming activities. Those with this kind of thought attend English as a Second Language (ESL) just because it is one of the obligations attached to their Cash Aid; they go for just spending their time because that is what the government needs them to do but they really don't go to acquire skills or knowledge. As life continues to be harder for them, they choose to relocate far from California in search for better places where they think life is a little cheaper than California. This is where they can find jobs and most of all where they can practice their activities they used to do from back their home countries.

Relocating to other states also exposes refugees to many problems including weather conditions which they difficultly do with. As said in earlier discussion, the air tickets which help refugees to come to the United States are given to them as travel loans and they must paid them back despite the circumstances. In fact, they start receiving payment reminders only two or three months after they are resettled in the country. Besides the air tickets which are given as travel loans, the loans acquired before travelling and the family support debts (especially for Africans with their so called African solidarity), refugees have to acquire other travel loans within the country. These other loans help them move or relocate from California to other states of the U.S. once they decide to move from California where the cost of living is very expensive according to them. They contact their friends and/or relatives who came to the country before them and who have secured jobs to lend money to use for their relocations to other states when life becomes hard for them in California. In addition to the loans stated above, refugees have to acquire more debts when it comes to paying their monthly rent dues as well as utility bills such as electricity, water, sewage, trash, phone among others. This happens because the cash aid given to them is always insufficient. For instance, an unemployed refugee who pays $1,550 rent per month receives $1,100 cash aid monthly. He/she will have to find ways to get the amount of $450 to cover this terrible shortfall every month. On top of that will be added an amount of $100 or more that they must pay as a penalty fee for late payment because it normally takes them time to find the amount to top up on the cash aid they receive from welfare services.

I have met with a refugee widow and an elderly in the same situation who disclosed the same information to me as I was conducting my research. Considering all these loans to which refugees are exposed, when can we think they will be able to pay back all the loans when we know that they have insufficient cash aid, they have to go to school to learn English language before they can start working and they have to wait long before they can find jobs? Moreover, many of them who have health issues neither work nor go to school and it takes many months for the Social Security Administration (SSA) to determine whether or not they are eligible for Social Security Income (SSI). In order to determine Social Security Income eligibility, refugees have to go through different medical examinations in various locations where their health claims are thoroughly checked by experienced healthcare service providers who will report to the Social Security Administration (SSA) for final decision before a sick or disabled refugee can start getting Social Security Income (SSI) which can help them in paying their bills including rent.

Here is a small scenario. Let us just consider that we are refugees and we are going through same problems as those described in the discussion above. How would life look like for us? As if that is not enough, we are refugees living under the same conditions, we open our mail box and we find different packages. When we open one of the envelops we find the following message: "As of 07/30/2017, the County is stopping your cash aid. Here's why:

You did not complete your annual renewal. Cash aid rules require an annual review to see if you can continue to get cash aid". Although this might be considered as a not a reality but just as a threatening letter to push the refugee to submit the report which was requested, this message can kill someone who is already living an uncertain life. It would be a great relief if those who understand the problems refugees went through in their countries of origin and in the settlement camps before they are resettled can do something or improve ways of helping the refugees in this country. Proper ways of assisting a needy person can help protect the person emotionally and psychologically, thus help avoid mental illnesses.

I am sorry. I have lived in this country for only 3 years now. I wonder if the county of San Diego, their contractors and resettlement agencies have ever taken time to research on the hardships refugees are going through in this country. I am pretty sure that these institutions are very much aware that the cash aid given to refugees is never enough to cover all their monthly expenses, how do they think the refugees cover these expenses? With a monthly deficit of over five hundred U.S dollars ($500) for someone who is not working is a terrible situation that refugee families will get out difficultly. They are being enforced into a deep financial hole!

To be sincere, with my personal analyze of this problem, I think that refugees might be involving in some unlawful activities which help them cover the gaps caused by their insufficient cash aid. Maybe this will be my next research topic because I still need to dig down to know how refugees cover the monthly expenses as their cash assistance does not help enough.

It would be another shameful situation if it happens that refugees can be involved in unlawful activities in order to raise money to help them cover their monthly expenses in a country where they were brought to rebuild their life. Is that how we can help someone rebuild his/her life after taking him/her from a refugee camp?

Bullying and Segregation in Schools and Social Places

According to Lewis Law Firm (n.d), an education law attorney, a single rude comment or physical incident may not be bullying. That said, a single physical or sexual attack may constitute some form of criminal conduct, and you should consider contacting the police. School bullying usually occurs when one or more people target a student and engage in a pattern of mean or rude comments, threats of physical or sexual violence, or actual physical or sexual violence. Bullying can be verbal comments, derogatory jokes, unwanted sexual advances, derogatory or defamatory entries on blogs, Facebook, Twitter or any other forum. Bullying can also take the form of physical or sexual assault. Bullying is terribly harmful to the victim and may result in serious physical and/or emotional health problems.

Refugee kids who enroll in public schools in the United States are faced with the challenge of being bullied and socially segregated while in the institutions. The intensity of bullying and seclusion has reached a point that even the teachers and other working staff in the schools are participants. As a result of these problems, the refugee children opt to leave school and stay at home where they have the protection of their parents and other family members. Other children who remain strong will keep going to school but have lost interest and think it is not the appropriate place for them to be. The problem of these children failing to attend school poses a major threat of losing an entire generation to illiteracy, poverty, crime, drug abuse, and ignorance (Schorshit, 2017). Parents become disappointed when they see their kids being harassed and tormented in schools yet; there is little they can do to help them. Many refugees in San Diego who have their kids in public schools have reported the trauma that these children undergo as a result of discrimination based on their origin and at times religion. It becomes challenging for them to concentrate in class because they always feel unwanted and out of place. Those who are not familiar with English are more traumatized than the others.

Children who are not conversant with the English language find it difficult to explain to their teachers when they are bullied in schools. They are enrolled in classes based on their age rather than abilities. However, it becomes impossible for them to cope in schools because teachers do not take their time to consult them about their progress. An additional problem is mounted by the fact that the parents may also lack the ability to help their children due to high illiteracy levels (Schorshit, 2017). Besides, these parents cannot communicate with school directors, principles and other responsible people in the schools and hence, the children either continue facing the humiliation or quit attending schools.

In 2016, I was volunteering and very much involved in helping with interpretation and translation during newcomer parents meetings in different Unified School Districts. This enabled me to understand what refugee children go through in schools in San Diego. Some teachers complained that X and Y children did not attend class a certain date whereas parents confirmed that the children left home for school that very date the teachers said. Many parents started asking themselves where do their children go if not to school? It is very simple to understand that the children leave home for school but they don't go to school because they fear to face discrimination or other bulling problems at school; and because they respect and fear their parents they decided to keep this for themselves. They know very well that due to illiteracy and language barriers facing their parents the latter will not be able to help them!

Recently in October 2017, I received a call from one of the most active New Neighbor Relief mentors who was assigned refugee children who study in El Cajon area. This mentor was called by the school as the family referee of the children. She was told by the school principal that a refugee child was involved in a fight with another student at school. The mentor asked me to help her to talk to the child's parents so that they can ask their child why she was involved in a fight at school. In order to understand the problem very well, I scheduled an appointment with the parent and asked to invite their child – the student – to the meeting. I went to their apartment and together we discussed with the child. She told us that she has been very patient but that day she felt very bad and could not refrain her emotions which led her to fight. When we asked her what was the exact reason why she fought; she told us that her classmate was used to show her a sign that she smells. She said most of the time the classmate could hold her arm and scratch is then showed her the sign of smell by putting fingers on the nose. These problems must be addressed by school principals and teachers to make sure refugee children are safe at school.

Refugees also face discrimination in other social places such as hotels, fast food cafés, and parks. It is common to find workers in these places secluding refugees and serving them last based on the idea that they may lack the required money to pay for the items. Furthermore, there is a rise of xenophobic attacks whereby the resettled refugees are attacked physically or by verbal abuse. Such cases have been reported in the streets of San Diego. However, the relevant authorities have failed to take the proper actions to ensure that the refugees are protected. As earlier discussed, the refugees have also found it problematic to access decent healthcare as a result of rampant racial discrimination against them.

We decided to raise this issue of bullying and segregation in schools because, during refugee parents – students meetings I participated in. I have heard about many situations of depression, anxiety, drop in grades, drop in attendance, psychosomatic symptoms, signs of physical confrontations such as cuts, torn clothes, bruises, pulled hair, loss of personal possessions, few friends, isolation, poor self-esteem, afraid to go to school...among refugee students and these elements are a proof of bullying is school. Refugee parents and refugee students are not trained or well informed about the steps to take against bullying activities.

Victims and their parents are generally unable to report these issues because of language barriers and the fear to be continued targets of the perpetrators and their families. Refugee parents don't even have an idea about the existence of education law attorneys who may be of help in such cases and even though they were informed about the existence of education law attorneys they would still not be able to contact them because of language barriers and lack of money to pay for the services.

This situation among others needs to be addressed before it becomes late. Parents and students need awareness about school bullying and a proper orientation regarding what to do when the refugee children are victims of bullying in school. If this kind of awareness and orientation cannot be done by resettlement agencies then Ethnic Community Based Organizations (ECBOs) should take the matter in hands.

Overcrowding and Disease Outbreaks

In San Diego, the majority of the refugees have been settled in the City Heights area. Over time, the number of refugees has continued to grow which has become a major concern due to the increased rate of communicable diseases. In such zones, the rate of water and airborne related diseases is high because of the close interaction between individuals. According to a report published by the Health Report (2012), these largely crowded refugee zones form a suitable breeding ground for diseases. The United Nations has also been at the forefront in pointing out the problem of disease spread in the highly congested refugee areas. Diseases such as malaria, jaundice, typhoid, and cholera are common in these areas due to poor sanitation. The incidence of epidemics in the areas has raised the alarm in the entire San Diego region. Efforts to reduce the number of people residing in the area have failed since this place offers an affordable livelihood to the refugees.

In the most populated refugee areas I am able to tell the hygienic conditions of the apartments just by passing in the neighborhood. I can feel horrible smells or odors. Lack of jobs and insufficiency of cash aid have played a big role in poor hygiene among refugee families. Many refugees keep dirt or un-washed clothes in their apartments for many days because of lack of money to do the laundry. More often other refugees especially the newcomers are not able to use the laundry machines and/or the laundry detergent. They are used to manually washing with bar soaps but now they have to face the machine to do the work. Only the refugee who receive orientation sessions and have a mentor come over to their apartment for visit have got a chance to be taught how to do different things including, but not limited to, laundry. The increase of poor hygienic conditions in apartments has also increased the existence of harmful insects such as bed bugs, cockroaches among others. These harmful insects cause severe body rashes to all family members in households.

Travel Bans

In the recent past, several policies and court precedents have been passed which has seen the decreased numbers of refugees being resettled in the United States (Parvini, 2017). Furthermore, some of the already relocated individuals have had their citizenship revoked based on the instituted policies. The travel bans have also been aimed at refugees from particular nations. These policies have had a spillover effect on some residents in San Diego. Other areas that are densely populated with refugees are now discourteous and unkind to the refugees from these countries (Parvini, 2017). The refugees are being harassed publicly with the resettlement agencies putting little efforts to address the issue. Such travel bans aimed at particular nations have resulted in strained relationships between the U.S and other countries. These travel bans and restrictions have left many refugees worried about their fate. Therefore, instead of going out in search of jobs to feed their families, some the refugees remain hidden in their houses.

Many refugees remain unsure or uncertain of what their situation will look like in the future with several policies and orders by the new administration in the country. They live under permanent fear of being deported at any time. The biggest problem in this situation is that there is not system put in place to help the existing refugees understand much about what travel bans mean and how they can be protected. I think there was supposed to be some kind of awareness sessions by either the resettlement agencies or other organizations assisting refugees in the country to help them understand more about these policies and orders but I have not seen or heard anything of that kind since the travel bans were put into place by the current administration. Refugees in the country are already suffering many problems as it is seen on the ground and efforts to address all these issues would be very highly appreciated.

This is another big problem which could increase the risk of mental health problem facing refugees in San Diego, California and, maybe, in other parts of the country.

Mental Health and Psychological Trauma

One of the issues that have been affecting refugees wherever they are placed in the United States of America and San Diego, California particularly is psychological trauma which brings complications in the mental health of the individuals. The main cause of the psychological torment is the separation of these people from their loved ones. After conflicts break out in their home countries, these people are forced to relocate to other places and become separated from their families and friends in the commotion. Therefore, settling in a strange place where they are unfamiliar with the residents, leads to the development of stress and depression (Brouwer & Rodwell, 2007). Furthermore, the problems they endure in the refugee camps before being resettled also contribute to the psychological trauma that they undergo. Also, the rejection of these individuals by the locals adds on to this burden. Culture conflicts are also causes of traumatic experiences that lead to depression and other mental illnesses among the refugees.

Brouwer and Rodwell (2007) reported that a majority of the refugees in the United States experienced psychological stress accompanied by physical dysfunction during the first few years of settlement. The researcher further noticed that during the subsequent years, the refugees try to increase their conformity to the new culture. These problems are still prevalent among the refugees settled in San Diego even after many years of living in the area. Many of these refugees hold onto the perception that conforming to the new culture will erode their culture. Furthermore, domestic violence among the homes of refugees accompanied by the drug and alcohol abuse in many homes also fuels the rise of mental problems. Despite these problems, the resettlement agencies have turned a blind eye to the situation. Besides, the refugees also fail to access the necessary services in medical facilities. However, the latter problem is promoted by the lack of sufficient funds to pay for therapy sessions and reduction of burdens increasing the problems.

Refugees are people who have gone through a lot before being resettled in developed countries. For this reason most refugees come when they are already suffering from one or more mental health problems such as emotional distress, depression, anxiety and trauma. Many of them suffer from Post Traumatic Stress Disorder (PTSD) in their countries of resettlement due to the life they lived in refugee camps and/or the circumstances they are exposed to in the countries where they are resettled.

I have realized that it might be possible that (in San Diego, California) problems associated to mental health and psychological trauma are, at some point, increased by the agencies or institutions assisting refugees. Let us take a moment and analyze the following mail received by a refugee household which had already acquired many debts because of insufficient cash aid: "This notice applies to: ABC John, Maria XYZ. Your eligibility to receive Medi-Cal will be discontinued the last day of 09/2017. The reason for this discontinuance is: You did not complete the redetermination process. In order to complete our review of your annual redetermination or change in circumstance, we needed the following information from you: ABC John and LMN Alice. We asked you for that information, but we have not received it and it is needed to complete your annual redetermination and process your change in circumstances. You can still get Medi-Cal, but you need to give us more information. We need it within 90 days, by 12/31/2017. We can give you Medi-Cal from 09/2017 if you are still eligible. If we do not get the information by 12/31/2017 you must reapply for Medi-Cal. If you are eligible for Medicare and your Medi-Cal eligibility is discontinued, this means that 09/2017 is the last month the State will pay your premium for supplementary insurance coverage (Part B Medicare). You will receive a written notice from the Social Security Administration, or you may call your Social Security district office if you have any questions about your Medicare status. If you have any questions about this action or if there are additional facts relating to your circumstances which you have not reported to us, please write or telephone. We will answer your questions or make an appointment to see you in person. Please remember that this action pertains to only the circumstances you reported to us, and that you may reapply at any time…/…"

Nobody in the household where this mail was received was able to read and write; everyone was illiterate. The head of the family tried his best to find help with reading the mail and understanding the message. I can imagine what happened to them when they got a chance to find someone to help them understand such a mail considering the fact that one or many members of that family were already suffering from one or more mental health problems. I can't imagine what mental illnesses combined with such a traumatic letter can lead to.

Earlier in September 2017, Nile Sisters Development Initiative (NSDI) invited us to attend the meeting of the Mental Health Coalition they started in early August. We attended this meeting and we desired to be part of this coalition as New Neighbor Relief – NNR. I was personally very excited to discuss this very sensitive topic with other many representatives from a various range of nonprofit organizations serving refugees in San Diego, California. We appreciated the idea of working as a coalition to mitigate mental health problems among refugees. I was still skeptical about the results this would reach considering the ways discussions were conducted and lack of funding to make this coalition a strong network on which refugees can rely to receive necessary care as far as mental health is concerned.

In my address to the audience, I first of all took an opportunity to thank NSDI for the great idea of starting such a coalition. I continued by mentioning clearly that we, New Neighbor Relief, shall not have time to waste in attending meetings which cannot lead to tangible results because we know that the hardships refugees are going through in San Diego, California. Most of the mental health problems here are a result of these hardships. Life is very hard for refugees in San Diego that it is not only difficult but also impossible for them to live a life without mental illnesses if those who have the powers to change this situation do not act as soon as possible. I shall not be tired of mentioning ultimately that when refugees are resettled to developed countries it is for the purpose of helping them rebuild their destroyed life. I wonder how they can start a new life in country where in lieu of resting mentally from what they went through in their respective countries and the refugee camps they continue developing mental illnesses.

My suggestion at this meeting was to stand as one organization and face law makers and/or decision makers in this part of the country to ask them to take necessary measures to solve refugee hardships which are the main cause of the development of mental illnesses. Other actions deployed by all the stakeholders (just like those already in place) can continue but this time we shall need to be sure that mental illnesses will be alleviated within the communities in San Diego, California. In that meeting on mental health coalition I continued to show to the audience that most of the causes of mental illnesses that many refugees are suffering from in San Diego can be mitigated if there is a political willingness. Many of the mental illnesses are due to hardships. Just a simple decision by the government can make a huge and considerable difference in addressing the issues of mental health among refugees.

For instance, the issues discussed about housing problems in this book whereby the refugees who pay $1,550 rent monthly receive cash aid of $1,100 every month. This is a family of 11 members and none of them has a job and they have a deficit of $450 every month just in rent fees apart from other many expenses they encounter every month. They borrow from friends and relatives who came to the country before them. Their friends and relatives have jobs and they promise them to pay back as soon as they get jobs; yet it takes them forever to find employment because they must learn English language before they can expect to get a job. Beside the deficit of $450 every month, these refugees have travel loans that they were given when they were granted resettlement by the government. They receive mails every month from the International Organization for Migration – IOM through the resettlement agencies asking them to pay back the travel loans they were given when they first came to the United States. This is just to name a few examples to show how families are suffering here restlessly. I believe that all the problems described in this book can find solutions if the government and their development partners put in more efforts, otherwise the efforts already deployed in assisting refugees will be worthless.

Access to Reproductive Healthcare Services

Access to reproductive and sexual health is both a critical need as well as a right for every woman. However, for the resettled refugees, women and girls are faced with the crisis of lack of proper reproductive health services. In many refugee stations and areas, this problem has been a leading cause of disease, disability, and death among girls and women of reproductive age. The resettlement agencies have failed to provide the minimum initial services package (MISP) to the refugee women and girls which have left them vulnerable. Cohen (2009) reports that initially, the federal government ensured that refugees could easily access reproductive health services, but the sudden cut in the funds dedicated towards this initiative weakened it and made the process impossible.

Furthermore, the United States also stopped contributing to the United Nations Population Fund (UNFPA) which derailed the access of reproductive health to displaced people living in the country. Despite the efforts by nonprofit organizations such as Catholic Charities, the demand for these services has overwhelmed them. Refugees, more so, women and teenage girls are prone to sexual abuse even after being resettled in the United States. Such heinous acts contribute to an amplified risk of contracting HIV, unwanted pregnancies, botched abortions, and risky childbirth among the teenagers (UNHCR, n.d). The lack of reproductive health services among the refugees has also led to the lack of family planning access. Therefore, some refugees have continued to sire more children even when they are not capable of raising them under the right conditions. However, this cannot be blamed on them since the access to reproductive health services has become limited.

According to Women's Refugee Commission Inc.(n.d), access to sexual and reproductive health (SRH) care is both a right and a critical need, yet in crisis situations—when vulnerabilities are drastically increased—lack of sexual and reproductive health care is a leading cause of death, disease, and disability among displaced women and girls of reproductive age. The Commission continues that the Minimum Initial Services Package (MISP) for Sexual and Reproductive Health in Crises provides the bare minimum for emergency response—and even this is not consistently implemented. Sexual and reproductive health services for all displaced women, men, and adolescents must extend beyond the MISP as a crisis stabilizes. The refugees in San Diego come from various places in the world where there have been all types of crisis. Many of them have never participated in Sexual and Reproductive Health from their home countries to the refugee camps. There is a great need to educate these refugees in San Diego about sexual and reproductive health in order to help them and their children live a better life tomorrow.

Yes, it is asserted that refugees in San Diego, California are living a horrendous life. From my findings, during my family visits, I realized that families with a big number of people are the neediest in San Diego. They are the most un-complaining families and it is true they are the ones with many survival problems. Many refugees from Africa especially have more than 5, 7, 9 children and they continue to produce more children without knowing what it takes to raise a large family in a developed country like the United States. They still have the same minds they used to have back in Africa where they could make as many children as possible because they were not sending children to school, they were not paying rent and other utility bills and life was not as very much expensive as it is the US. However, many other refugees in San Diego, whether they are from Africa or from other countries, would like to be educated and learn more about sexual and reproductive health.

Sexual and reproductive health is not only refugee parents' business but the youth also are a target of the consequences that may arise from the lack of information on sexual and reproductive health. If we can remember that the majority of refugee children were born in horrible life conditions in refugee camps where their parents lived for over 20 years (for most African refugees) we can understand the need for the youth to be informed and/or educated about sexual and reproductive health. This education process would be very much helpful to these people to avoid early pregnancies, unwanted pregnancies, risky abortions and sexual transmittable infection including, but not limited to, HIV/AIDS.

It has been remarked also that refugee teenagers need to learn a lot more about sexual and reproductive health. On these skills on sexual and reproductive health I can add hygiene skills among menstruating refugee girls. In schools where refugee children are enrolled their classmates complain about emissions of horrible odors by those who are at their menstruating age. Refugee girls need to be trained in hygiene skills and how to handle their menstruation periods while attending classes. However, I realized that some parents know how to guide their daughters in menstruating age but they lack necessary means to support their daughters because they don't have jobs and the Cash Aid they receive in never enough to help refugee families take care of all their situations and the food stamps can only buy food items (and not all because restricted)... and cannot buy pads for their mature daughters during their menstruation periods.

Education, information or awareness on Sexual and Reproductive Health is critically important among refugees in San Diego, California and the United States at large. During my research on "The multifaceted management problems of refugee resettlement in the United States of America (USA); I had a chance to meet and discuss more with refugees with a focus to those from the Democratic Republic of Congo (DRC). It is actually this research that I developed into a book when I realized that there was more to be told and informed about refugee life in San Diego, California. From my discussions, questions and answers (Q&A) sessions we got to know that while in refugee camps, refugees who resettled in the U.S in the past communicate with those in the refugee camps and advise them that life is very hard in the U.S for those who do not have many children. They deceived them that they should produce many children so that they can be given much attention and money to care for their families upon their arrival to the United States. They were told that the more children a family has the more money it is given at the end of every month. For this reason many refugees give birth in average to 2 children in 2.5 years in the camps. They don't know the problems them and their children can face in the future if they continue to bear unplanned children.

All these horrible situations can be eradicated or at least mitigated if there is a real and true willingness to help people overcome them.

Lack of Information about Public Health Issues

The majority of refugees, who are resettled in San Diego, and in the United States at large, come from the developing nations. Therefore, the condition of living in their country of origin and that in the United States is different. The fact that these people are not enlightened about the public health issues just aggravates the situation. The manner in which they dispose of their garbage is a major cause of concern. In the areas where refugees live, it is common to find garbage being thrown in and around the houses, which makes their living conditions unbearable (Gushulak, Weekers, & MacPherson, 2009). However, while people may want to blame the resettled refugees for such conditions, the root of the problem is that these people fail to be familiar with the public health regulations. They come to the country with very little to no knowledge about public health. They have no idea at all about how to improve the health of their families and communities by promoting healthy lifestyles, preventing disease, and removing environmental dangers.

Furthermore, as reported by Leaning, Spiegel, and Crisp (2011), the responsible humanitarian agencies have failed in resource allocation and service delivery aimed at educating refugees about observing the recommended public health policies. The researchers further established that the issue of public health disparity faced by these individuals can be blamed on poor decision-making and resource-allocation by the responsible parties. Personal hygiene and cleanliness among these individuals is also another public health issue that continues to torment them.

In many apartments visited, I found food particles disseminated almost everywhere in the apartments. Trash canes exude terrible odors and it becomes really difficult to spend more than 10 minutes in some of these apartments because of these unbearable smells. Families who have got a change to be assigned a mentor by New Neighbor Relief – NNR don't have many of these problems because the mentors teach them different topics including public health issues. It is unfortunate that many families don't have mentors because, despite the commitment to serve the refugees with love, NNR is very short of resources to take care of more refugee families than it is doing now. Yet the needs are increasing in the community.

Many refugees in San Diego, California spend most of their time checking plastic bottles and other recyclable containers in the dumpsters in the areas where they live with the hope of collecting as many containers as possible that they can sell and get some money to help them pay their utility bills. They have other household expenses in addition despite their insufficient Cash Aid they receive from the government welfare service. This is, by no means, a very big problem of Public Health. When they check in the dumpsters they don't care about covering their hands or noses yet there is a lot of dirt in there and the smells or odors are insupportable. Their focus is always on collecting as many recyclable containers as they can because the more containers the more money is paid by recycle companies.

At New Neighbor Relief – NNR, we receive tens of calls from refugees every day requesting help with transportation to take their collected containers to the recycle companies in the city and around. NNR has tried hard to explain to some of the refugees the dangers they are running through in visiting dumpsters and trash canes every day searching for recyclable containers and bottles. Unfortunately, refugees show that they cannot stop because they have many bills to pay every month and the Cash Aid received from the government welfare services is never enough to help them pay for these bills. Yet many are jobless and they are uncertain when they will be able to secure jobs.

Recycle companies are doing good business. They take advantage of the existence of refugees, homeless people and other poor and unemployed people to get recyclable containers and/or bottles to grow their business in San Diego.

I am still not so sure if they even care about the health of their clients who bring business to them.

This is again a situation which can be avoided just by helping those involved in collecting plastic contains and bottles to improve their life conditions and be able to pay those bills pushing their noses in dumpsters and trash canes every day. However, my purpose of writing this book was – just like the book's title reads – to help people understating the multifaceted management problems of refugee resettlement in the United States of America. I did this only in order to attract the attention of people in the community and possibly reaching out to decision makers to help for a change in order to make the United States a better place to live for everyone. I am not a misfortune prophet but I can say that if, in the upcoming 10 years, nothing is done about the problems I have researched; the United States may be a victim of a demon of its own creation. By not assisting the refugees in a proper way, the country is unknowingly placing bombs on the streets which will explode one day in the future.

All these issues are critically serious among refugee families and I totally understand the need of refugee education on public health issues for the benefit of their families, their neighbors and the whole communities in which they live.

Increased Crime Rates

The continuous influx of refugees in San Diego has raised major concerns about the crime rate in the area. Most of these neighborhoods where the refugees resettle, such as City Heights, have been experiencing an increase in the rate of crime since the 2000s as reported by Burks (2014). In this case, the refugees are both the affected as well as the perpetrators of the act. A significant proportion of the refugees tends to engage in criminal activities as a result of being jobless. The insufficiency of the cash aid from the government and partner agencies has also been a major contributor of the refugee engagement in crime. On the other hand, residents perceive that the agencies give the resettled refugees huge checks and therefore, they try to steal the money from these individuals even when they have nothing in their pockets.

Burks (2014) conducted a brief survey in the City Heights area and found that the resettled individuals felt that the responsible agencies have neglected them despite the fact that they have not accessed reliable jobs. Therefore, these people have to find alternative methods of providing for their families. In many instances, these methods are crime-related. The crime rates established in these neighborhoods are far above the average city rate. It has been reported that in the refugee areas, the rate averages are 40 crimes per 1000 people while San Diego's average falls at 26 crimes per 1000 individuals (Burks, 2014). Creating more initiatives to fight against joblessness or idleness in the area would be a great remedy for these increased crime rates. Another remedy for this would be educating or training the youth on responsible leadership for them to understand the roles tomorrow's life holds for them.

For instance, initiating youth activities which could fight idleness, depression, anxiety, drug abuse, conflict, prostitution and lack of integration in the community – to create a collaborative space – would be a good fit to combat youth involvement in crimes in San Diego. A space that youth can use to connect, share, resolve conflicts, and innovate ways to improve their lives.

Once such activities are established, many youth will come to participate. This can create even an opportunity to engage many more youth in the community on important health, and social issues. The youth-led groups can share information about HIV/AIDS, Sexual Gender Based Violence, Human Rights, and Women's Empowerment topics to name a few. Additionally, these activities can create multiple opportunities for youth to grow in their leadership and teambuilding skills. With youth leaders at the forefront of the initiatives, other youth will be inspired to be involved and the community will develop a respect for the youth population as change makers and contributors of society. At this point, the youth will be looked at in the community like responsible change makers instead of crime perpetrators.

These ideas were originally adopted by New Neighbor Relief - NNR as one of the ways to help for a true and sustainable way to contribute to refugee youth integration in San Diego. The organization dreams of eradicating youth involvement in crimes was to create Refugee Youth-led teams (boys and girls), organize them, equip them, train them, and give them opportunity to play tournaments with prizes to win. It would offer great opportunities to learn many things about HIV/AIDS, Sexual Gender Based Violence, Human Rights, and Women's Empowerment topics... Unfortunately, it looks like NNR has just plenty of community development project ideas but very limited funding to implement them.

On the other hand, the increase of crimes can be caused by the lack of respect of human rights by government services themselves, especially the right to life. We have a large number of asylum seekers in the country who are also neglected yet they are also human beings who came to the country in search for protection of their life. Here I am talking about asylum seekers who are already allowed to work and whose work permits have expired. This is a group of people who suffer a lot in this country even more than the refugees because refugees are crying but at least they have some support from the government although it is not as enough as they would wish. I would not go far in this matter considering its sensitivity but I can remind those who would like to understand that asylum seekers are also suffering so much in San Diego, California and the hardships under which they live can lead them to participation in organized crimes in order to find means of living.

This can be explained by the fact that asylum seekers who are not yet allowed to work in the country have no support. They can be given emergency food stamp for only thirty (30) day and an emergency healthcare insurance called "restricted medical insurance". I am hopeful that my readers can understand what means a restricted insurance. Once their work permits are expired they have to wait up to minimum three (3) months before their work permits can be renewed. As I mentioned earlier, when I analyzed the difficulties to access employment; asylum seekers cannot work during the renewal process of their work permits. If a work permit expires while an asylum seeker is working, the employer has to stop him/her from working to avoid problems with the Internal Revenue Service – IRS because there is no way the employee can pay taxes if not allowed to work in the country. Once a work permit expires, automatically the expired driver's license cannot be renewed; therefore an asylum seeker whose work permit has expired has no right to movement – no right to life in this country.

Human Trafficking Activities

Human trafficking is viewed as the new form of slavery in the contemporary world. Human trafficking involves the forceful acquisition of men, children, and women who are then forced into labor. Refugees are often lured into human trafficking through enticing promises such as good jobs with attractive salaries. Children are vulnerable because of their marginalization in the contemporary world (McCarthy, 1998). Also, women have also been another group that has been hit by trafficking. Human trafficking victims are forced into immoral acts such as prostitution, drug trafficking, and forced labor. A trafficked individual is forced to the conditions of modern slavery that include involuntary servitude, peonage, and coercive labor terms.

In the United States, human trafficking has been on the increase among the refugees due to the desperation and the need for a better life. The U.S Department of State has reported that in the country, refugees, more so women, are highly impacted by human trafficking. The traffickers easily lure women as a result of their illiteracy, unfamiliar with the English language, neglect by their husbands, and failure to familiarize with the United States labor laws and regulations. Furthermore, many refugees prefer to work in jobs that are hidden from the public domain and are unregulated by the government. The federal government has outlined some reasons that contribute to the increased influx of refugees being trafficked. These include:

- The discrimination against women
- Religious discrimination
- Lack of political support for the resettled refugees
- High poverty levels
- Deception of a better life

While the federal and state governments have imposed strict regulations against those people that are found to conduct human trafficking, the current statistics indicate that trafficking has been on the increase. More so, these traffickers target areas such as the City Heights where they are sure to lure hundreds of desperate refugees. The law enforcers have failed to restrict such inhumane actions. Some of these enforcers have been blamed for being biased and neglecting the refugees who are also new members of the society.

Neglect of the Elderly Refugees

According to Keselly (2002), elderly refugees are at a higher risk of severe human rights abuse as well as being in need of physical care. Furthermore, this group of refugees also undergoes a lot of psychological trauma as a result of being displaced from their homes. After being resettled in California, the United States, the elderly refugees fail to be given the necessary attention and care that they need. Some of these people do not have anyone to care for them after being separated from their loved ones. They are left to depend on the little cash aid extended to them by the agencies and other humanitarian organizations. The elderly refugees cannot seek for jobs which leave them entirely dependent on these donations. Those who are lucky to live with their family members also suffer a similar fate. They are left alone at home to care for themselves while the rest of the family members go out in search of jobs and attend schools (Keselly, 2002). Therefore, these people are left with no supervision at all nor a caretaker to watch over them. It is a common phenomenon to find the elderly being prone to diseases at any time. As a result, many elderly refugees have succumbed to diseases due to the lack of concern by the relevant authorities.

Furthermore, these refugees, especially those living alone, are faced with the problem of transport and communication. First, they cannot drive and at the same time, accessing public transportation is also difficult for them. Using cell phones is also a major problem among this population, and therefore, in times of emergency, they are unable to call for help. Even though the problems being experienced by these elderly refugees are widely prevalent in the San Diego region, there have been minimal efforts in trying to address the issue.

For instance, many elderly refugees from the Democratic Republic of Congo (DRC) between the ages of 70-85 living in San Diego are left alone as their family members go to ESL classes, to work and/or to school. Nobody takes care of them at all. The time they are left alone without supervision is sufficient enough for them to develop more mental health issues. There is need to take measures that protect these people from developing thoughts that will cause them more health problems. These elderly refugees have either lost the majority or their family members during the war in their countries and others among them left more of their children in refugee camps in Africa. Knowing that their children cannot visit or see them soon affects their mental life as well.

Another problem which affects the life of elderly refugees in San Diego, and I am afraid it might be affecting elderly refugees across the United States, is the loan they were given by the International Organization for Migration (IOM) in partnership with the United Nations High Commission for Refugees (UNHCR) for their air tickets at the time they travelled to the United States. Every refugee is supposed to work to reimburse their travel loan money once they are resettled in the U.S. The question the elderly refugees asked me during one of my interviews was: "How did they think someone old of my age would be able to reimburse the air ticket loan?" (Asked an elderly refugee aged about 79).

If those bringing refugees in the country could be merciful, they could have considered the problems these refugees faced in their home countries, their age groups and the fact that they cannot attend school to learn English as a Second Language (ESL) or be able to work to refund these travel loans.

Another elderly refugee told me that before coming to the United States he was told that his air ticket was free and he will not pay it back. He was very surprised that mail was coming every month to ask him to pay back the ticket amount. He said that he spends days and nights thinking about that problem. He cannot work due to his age and he has no other income besides the little Social Security Income (SSI) which does not even cover his monthly expenses.

I think that a fee waiving of the ticket loans given to refugees would be a great relief especially to these elderly refugees who cannot work. It would reduce the cases of mental illnesses among them. Strategies to take care of the elderly refugees would also positively impact their life greatly. At a certain age, a person needs more than just food, clothing and medical care. Taking them to places where they can release stress and stop thinking about the hardship that their children are going through would be a pathway to a solution.

On the same topic, we have met another refugee elderly woman from the Democratic Republic of Congo (RDC) who was supposed to be 78 years old but her age was miscalculated by officers in the refugee camps in Tanzania. They recorded 54 years instead. Because her husband is 79, he was eligible for Social Security Income (SSI) but his wife was not eligible and she was referred to Welfare To Work program to learn English as a Second Language (ESL) and search for job thereafter. This refugee woman is very sick and old enough, she cannot work. She is old and as tired as her husband. She showed her Identification (ID) card from her country, the DR Congo, when it was still Zaire during the time of President Joseph Désiré Mobutu (Sese Seko Kuku Ngbendo Wa Za Banga) the great dictator. This ID card is an old authentic and true one that every old Congolese should have. The name and picture of the husband are affixed in the ID and the date of their marriage as well as the names of their children. This story, like many other refugee stories, was shocking. I asked her to give me her original ID card so that we could go meet Catholic Charities representatives because she was resettled in the United States by this agency. I went to Catholic Charities in San Diego together with Dan Collins, President of NNR, and we had a long discussion with of the managers. Unfortunately, we were told that there is nothing the resettlement agency can do to help this sick old refugee woman modify her wrong age to the correct one. Who else would be able to help a refugee in such a situation if the resettlement agency which brought her to the country cannot help?

We are still looking for a solution to this problem. If anyone among the readers out there has an idea about this, please do not hesitate to contact us. Simply send an email to: newneighbor.relief@gmail.com or info@congolesefamily.org and your help will be very much appreciated.

Domestic Violence (DV)

Domestic abuse, or domestic violence, generally refers to violence between adults, especially between spouses (Legal Match, n.d). Domestic abuse can be either physical or psychological (i.e., threats, degrading language). In most states, the term domestic abuse refers to any conduct that causes or threatens to cause injury between: family members, spouses, residents of the same household.

Child abuse is sometimes excluded from the term domestic abuse, as this is considered its own category. However, any form of violence against a family member is treated seriously and is punished very strictly under state and federal laws.

Legal Match continued that Domestic Violence has many consequences. Domestic Violence cases often involve a number of criminal charges, including assault, battery, sexual assault, and rape. If criminal charges are brought against the offender, it can result in criminal penalties such as a jail or prison sentence, as well as monetary fines.

In addition to criminal penalties, the person who is found guilty of domestic abuse may also face other legal consequences, such as:

- *Damages:* The defendant may have to pay monetary damages to cover the financial losses of the victim (such as hospital bills or pain and suffering)
- *Restraining orders:* A judge can issue a domestic abuse injunction such as a temporary or permanent restraining order. These can require the defendant to stay a certain distance from the victim, and can prohibit communication with the victim.
- *Rehabilitation courses:* A judge can also require the defendant to attend mandatory rehabilitation courses, such as anger management classes.
- *Custodial rights:* The defendant may lose their rights to child custody and visitation. This is true even if the charges involved spousal abuse, since courts aim to protect children from being exposed to violence.
- *Loss of various rights:* Serious instances of domestic abuse can even result in the loss of various rights, such as the right to own a firearm, and the right to have a driver's license.

On the same note by Legal Match, Domestic Violence victim is affected in different ways. It can also result in various legal effects on the victim or victims. A single instance of domestic abuse can often have dramatic effects on the lives of those involved in the incident. The assistance of a lawyer may sometimes be required to help the victim deal with the legal issues that may result after a domestic abuse incident.

One of the main effects is a change in child custody and visitation orders. The defendant may lose their child custody rights, and they may be prohibited from visiting the child. While this is often for the protection of the child, it also means that the child will not be able to contact their parent for some period of time, or even permanently.

Also, domestic abuse often results in the victims being relocated out of state or to a shelter home, again for the protection of the victim. This is common if the domestic abuse involves instances of harassment or stalking, or if the defendant has previously violated a restraining order. In some cases the defendant may be liable for the costs involved in physically relocating the victim.

Lastly, domestic abuse can often result in severe emotional trauma for the victim, as well as witnesses to the violent conduct. A judge may then recommend that the victim and/or witnesses attend counseling or rehabilitation sessions. Domestic abuse is a very serious matter, and can have various legal effects on both the offender and the victims. Even witnesses may become legally involved in a domestic abuse case. Recurring instances of domestic abuse should be reported to authorities immediately (Legal Match, n.d).

In San Diego, refugees involved in Domestic Violence cases are not aware of the process, the consequences and what will happen next for themselves and their families because they are not trained, skilled and most of those involved are not educated enough to understand the laws of the country.

Domestic Violence is real and multifaceted among refugee families in San Diego. During my research period, I have focused mostly on Domestic Violence (DV) among refugee families from the Democratic Republic of Congo (DRC) in San Diego. In these families have been recorded multifaceted cases of Domestic Violence including, but not limited to, same-sex domestic violence, violence and/or abuse by mother, father, sister-in-law and/or by natal family members, sexual abuse that can include marital rape, being forced to watch and imitate pornographic acts, extreme sexual neglect, economic abuse and isolation from family and friends, battering during pregnancy, etc.

We cannot separate Domestic Violence from lack of Peaceful Cohabitation if we really need to eradication the problems in a sustainable way and help the refugees from the DRC and others from the African Great Lakes region live peacefully and without involving in crimes in this country.

In August 2017, Mid-City Police Department (830's service area) called a meeting after reports showed that many refugees from the Democratic Republic of Congo (DRC) were the most people involved in Domestic Violence (DV) in San Diego. The meeting involved all agencies working with refugees to discuss the DV issues among Congolese refugees. As a representative of New Neighbor Relief at this meeting, I showed that the right way to eradicate DV among these refugees is to have them participate 100% in the process for a sustainable management of the problem in order to reach zero DV case in the upcoming months. After this meeting I decided to bring all Congolese refugees together so as to fight DV together. Because there was no traditional Congolese Community organization in San Diego, I created the Congolese Family Support Steering Committee (CFSSC) to start working to fight against DV and to prepare the foundation for a well organized Congolese Community organization in San Diego.

Ethnic tribes' leaders who were gathered to lead the CFSSC decided to change the name as it was a bit difficult to pronounce by the majority of the members. The members present at the fourth meeting decided changed the name of the organization from CFSSC to CFSO (Congolese Family Support Organization) which is being registered as a Community Based Organization (CBO). The CFSO will serve for the very first time as a reference for every Congolese refugee family in need of support of any kind and guidance in many ways. Now CFSO has the support of all Congolese refugees from all ethnic groups represented in San Diego, New Neighbor Relief (NNR), Congolese led churches, Mid-City Police Department, Price Philanthropies, Family Justice, Survivors of Torture, Alliance for African Assistance... but still lack necessary funding to operate like other Ethnic Community Based Organizations from other countries serving their members in San Diego, California.

According to the Congolese representatives at the meeting organized by Mid-City Police Department on Domestic Violence (DV), there are many problems causing their involvement in DV. Among the causes he listed: lack of jobs, poor housing, poverty in families, insufficient Cash Aid, restrictions attached to food stamps, difficult access to transportation, difficult access to welfare and healthcare services due to poor interpretation and/or translation services, lack of an organized Congolese community to guide them, undermining Congolese refugee skills, lack or poor orientation, lack of understanding of laws, insufficient household items and clothing, ESL program not meeting the needs of refugees from Africa (especially those from the DR Congo where French is the official language), locked systems making refugee life harder, etc. All those elements have highly contributed to persistence of problems among the refugees in San Diego including Domestic Violence. The war conflict background of the countries of origin has also played a major role in lack of peaceful cohabitation among these people and the main purpose why refugees are resettled in this country (starting a new life) cannot become a reality when all these problems are observed in the community.

Refugees and immigrants who come from the African Great Lakes Region have experienced many war conflicts and sometimes they or their relatives back home might have been somehow involved in the conflicts that made people lose their belongings, family members and flee their countries.

Once resettled in the United States (San Diego) they look at each other with a lot of apathy causing hate among them silently. I suspect this to be the reason why there are many organized refugee communities in San Diego but there has never been an organized Congolese community. War conflicts history prevents Africans from this region to interact easily with one another. This situation may cause serious issues which can negatively affect the efforts to help refugees start a new life in the United States. In the same process of helping refugees start a new life in the United States, Domestic Violence and other conflicts must be mitigated or eradicated among them.

In San Diego, refugees from Africa, most especially the refugees from the Democratic Republic of Congo are more involved in Domestic Violence. In many parts of Africa a man can hit his wife or his child without issues and they will continue to live together after the incidence. Back in their home countries, because the laws there are not reinforced, Domestic Violence is dealt with in using culture or tradition beliefs. The fact that the laws of their countries are not enforced to the extent of punishing those involved in Domestic Violence deceives them. They tend to think they can continue doing the same thing in the United States where they are granted resettlement without knowing that it is punishable by the laws of the country.

On the other hand, it was observed that in many refugee families (for those who have jobs) the husband or the wife sends money to Africa to help family members who remained in the refugee camps. This is done without the arrangements between household partners and domestic abuses start imme-diately once one of them realizes that money transfers were done or are being done without informing the other partner. This is another issue arising in refugee households in San Diego. Other Congolese men have reported that they are simply victims of problems that occurred long time ago in their house-holds when they were still back in their home countries or in refugee settle-ments. "We don't know where these cases of Domestic Violence will take us because some women are now making their husband to pay. If they made them upset in the past before they were granted resettlement or if their husband had slapped them in the past and no one intervened to help them out; now our wives know that the secret is simply to call 911 and the man will be arrested and later there will be a restraining order" (said a refugee from the DRC).

There is a high need to deal with Domestic Violence issues among refugees in San Diego. Preventive measures would be very much appreciated and would be the right way to help fight DV problems. We know already that most of the refugees involved in domestic abuse cases are those who are not educated and/or who don't know about the consequences and how the law deals with Domestic Violence cases. Why not train them? Why not help them to be aware of all the consequences that await the victims and the perpetrators of Domestic Violence before it is late? Large awareness is highly needed in this area to help refugee understand what the law says about DV in the country.

I think it is good to fight Domestic Violence through organized refugee com-munities where they can speak the same language. Creating spaces where refugee communities can meet and discuss the problem affecting them and their families in San Diego would be one of the great ways to deal with Domestic Violence among refugee families. Training and/or awareness sessions with emphasize on the consequences associated to Domestic Violence can be organized within the refugee communities for a sustainable solution.

CONCLUSION

In summing up, it is evident that the resettled refugees in San Diego face many challenges that negatively impact their stay and make it difficult for them to start a new life in the United States. The refugees leave their country as a result of heated conflicts that arise motivated by political conflicts, ethnic disparities, religious differences, and natural calamities such as famine. Initially, refugees may seek assistance from neighboring countries, but when their population grows, they are forced to move in far off nations. When conditions in their countries of origin fail to stabilize, the refugees seek resettlement in a third country. Mostly, the third countries are the developed ones such as the United States. Those who are accepted to resettle in the U.S undergo a strict security check to ensure that only those who are in dire need are resettled. San Diego has been one of the regions in the United States that have been flocked by re-settled refugees and holds the largest population of resettled people in the California as well as nationwide.

At different meetings, I was given opportunities to speak about issues affecting refugees in San Diego, California but these were very short time opportunities of five to fifteen minutes. These opportunities were given to me at different events were there was San Diego Refugee Forum members, Mid-City Police Department, KPBS, San Diego Union Tribune, Mind Mental Health Coalition members etc. During these events, it was difficult to talk about all the problems affecting refugees in the United States. I am very happy to come up with this book which gives me an opportunity to speak without looking on the watch. It helps me to express myself freely to help others know about these issues and see how they can help either in mitigating or eradicating them.

Typical management problems of resettlement that refugees in San Diego face include reduced cash aids, mental health and psychological trauma, lack of reproductive health services, transport issues, language barriers, unwelcoming communities, mental health issues and psychological trauma, human trafficking, and neglect of the elderly among others. Furthermore, discrimination and bullying in public spaces are also other problems that these refugees deal with on a daily basis. Therefore, the resettlement agencies, federal and state governments, and other responsible authorities must develop possible solutions to eradicate or at least mitigate these problems to ensure that these refugees in San Diego, California and the United States as a whole have a comfortable and secure life.

I remind here that the only reason refugees are resettled in developed countries is to help them start a new life after what they went through in their home countries. But from what I have found about refugees' life in San Diego, California; it would be truly a daydream to think that refugees can start a new life in the United States if the problems described in this book are not taken care of accordingly. Each of these problems affects the lives of the refugees in one way or another while all the problems, at the same time, are a brake to the development of the entire communities. Many more efforts are needed from all settings to stop what is already and may continue to be disgusting if nothing is done.

Like I said already in the previous discussions, by bringing all these problems affecting refugees in San Diego to the knowledge of the public, I have done my part. It is up to each and everyone among my readers and anyone else who will get a chance to hold this book in their hands to do their part. That is the only way to make San Diego, California and the United States a better place for everyone.

Maybe the answer is for each of us to choose one thing to fix and not let go. Take a small piece of the refugee injustices and make it your responsibility. Whether it means agitating for more cash assistance from California government officials; advocating for more support and community meeting places for refugee youth to gather or adopting a refugee family and becoming a mentor to them... and not only for this year – but next year too. Because that is what it is going to take to start to heal these refugees' suffering. A ground swell of efforts put together by our small individual actions. That is what made America great and we can do it again for our new neighbors from other lands.

In this book, most of the examples about the challenging refugee life are talking about the refugees from the Democratic Republic of Congo. I must confess that this does not mean that those from the DR Congo suffer more than other refugees in California and the United States at large. Examples were focused on the refugees from DR Congo because I was able to find more information from them as I know all the languages spoken by these refugees. I had no funding to conduct my research and that is why I did not consider to interview other refugee groups as it would involve interpretation services and other services to be paid for.

Finally, I thank all the readers for considering to understand, and share with others, the multifaceted management problems of refugee resettlement in (San Diego, California) the United States and most of all for taking action to make the country a better place to live for everyone. Please feel free to contact me should you have any question about this book or should you have any idea on how you can help in one or more of the problems discussed in this book for the betterment of refugee life in San Diego, California and the United States in general.

Thank you to all!

ABOUT THE AUTHOR

Prof. Justin B. Mudekereza is a national of the Democratic Republic of Congo (DRC). He fled his country in 2006 as a result of physical torture after elections. He is an icon known for his many efforts for social justice, human rights, and development in many African countries. He is a person who does not keep quiet or stand and watch when people are suffering around him. From a bigger family of 44 children of his late father, he learned to make peace, to share with others and most of all to fight for others whenever they are victims of injustice of any kind.

Although it is a bit difficult to talk about a person who has given all his time and strength helping others; we can try to talk about his greater and very remarkable achievements on 3 different levels: in the RD Congo, in other parts of Africa and in the United States of America.

- **In the DR Congo**

In 1998 a fatal war started in the country between the government and rebels groups also known as the African World War. It made millions of people lose their live and belongings. A year later, he created the "Comité d'Encadrement des Femmes et des Enfants – Veuves et Orphelins (CEFEVO), an nonprofit organization which helped widows, orphans and vulnerable children, women victims of rape and other many war victims in Sounth Kivu region. Under his management, the organization won many funding contracts with many international organizations and the United Nations organizations agencies such as UNFAO, UNWFP and UNDP. This achievement earned him the trust of the local community to the extent where he was considered as a threat to some politicians in the country.

He participated in the creation of the "Conseil des Organisations de Femmes Agissant en Synergie – COFAS" a women's rights movement which played a great role in search for peace during the war in the country and he worked actively with other many organizations of the civil society.

In recognition of his efforts, community members decided to form a foundation under his name. Today, the Justin Mudekereza Foundation (www.jmudekfoundation.org) assists orphans and vulnerable children (OVC), widows and other needy people in South Kivu province. The foundation emphasizes child education as this sector was abandoned by the government long time ago.

- **In other parts of Africa**

In late 2007, after surviving torture, Prof. Justin fled to Uganda and arrived in Kampala in mid 2008. He suffered to find a place to stay, just like other many refugees in the country. Later he was granted refugee status by Ugandan authorities who gave him a letter to go settle into a refugee camp. Considering the political issues in his country of origin, and the fact that his country is bordering Uganda and not far from the refugee camp; he declined the settlement offer and decided to stay in Kampala the capital city of Uganda.

While in Kampala, he realized that there were also very many development challenges the same way it was in the Democratic Republic of Congo (DRC). He founded and registered Aspire for African Development & Consulting Limited – ADEC LTD (www.adeconsult.net), a development oriented consulting company which assisted different Community Based Organizations (CBOs) in their work of fighting against poverty. He started discussions with community members and mobilized them to fight against various development problems observed in the community. This included street children, environmental cleanness to fight against malaria, early child marriages, early child pregnancies, HIV/AIDS and other Sexually Transmittable Infections – STI among others. In this initiative with some Ugandans he created Community Development Vision – CDV which is now a nationwide nongovernmental organization helping people in Uganda (facebook @CDV uganda).

As an Independent Consultant, he helped in organizing and fundraising for Change African Child International – CACI (www.cac-international.org) a non-governmental organization assisting orphans and vulnerable children in Ugandan suburbs. While guiding several community organizations in Uganda; he was hired as a college teacher at Namasuba College of Commerce – NCC (www.namasubacollege.com), Makerere Institute of Business and Management (MIBM) and worked as a Consultant at NNC Consulting. With a desire to serve in other parts of Africa, he got another teaching job at PIDAM University in Bosaso Somalia, Puntland State, where he taught from 2014-2015 before moving to the United States of America. He also helped as a Consultant at Badbaado Umbrella (YouTube: BADBAAD UMBRELLA) a non-governmental organization working to fight HIV/AIDS in the Puntland State of Somalia with the partnership of the United Nations Development Program (UNDP).

In Kenya, he participated in the creation of Ndima Women Against Poverty (NWAP) a Community Based Organization (CBO) which mobilizes and supports women to fight against poverty in Karatina, Nyeri (Facebook @Ndima Women Against Poverty – NWAP).

Back in Uganda in late 2015, he was hired as Project Coordinator by a non-profit organization. In partnership with the government of Uganda and the Ugandan based organization which sent him to a training in Los Angeles, California. Unfortunately, due to the continued threats, he felt unsafe to go back to Uganda and decided to seek asylum in the United States. The name of the organization was not listed because of his current asylum status.

- **In the United States of America**

With the desire to serve the underprivileged in the community, Prof. Justin started working as volunteer at Alliance for African Assistance as an interpreter/translator. He helped his fellow African refugees communicate with their Case Managers. Later on, other institutions and/or organizations such as International Rescue Committee (IRC), San Diego Unified School Districts, Say San Diego etc. requested his help as an interpreter/translator in San Diego, California. During this volunteering time, he started to comprehend how refugees were assisted in San Diego and the challenges affecting them in the country. He felt the need to do more as his own contribution to the betterment of refugee life…

Upon reception of his work permit, Justin started hunting jobs from every corner in San Diego but couldn't find any as soon as he hoped. He was like other refugees and asylum seekers in the area. Access to jobs is not easy for newcomers in San Diego no matter the level of education, experience or skills earned outside the United States! After going through several job interviews and despite his level of education from back home, his experience in the non-profit sector; he soon realized the need to go back to school in a U.S university to earn another degree. Because of lack of resources he decided to take a few training, find part time jobs and save money for studies. He then got trained in Mental Health Interpretation and Mental Health First Aid. He took course for a verified certificate in Project Management at the University of Adelaide in Australia.

He got hired by San Diego State University (SDSU) as teacher in a LARC project, later by Language trainers USA and Wyzant tutoring. He continued private tutoring of French and Swahili languages to individuals interested in learning these languages. He decided to enroll at the Atlantic International University - AIU (USA) where he earned a Master's degree of Science in Project Management and currently enrolled in a Doctorate (Ph.D) program in the same field. His dream is to continue his teaching career while he contributes to development initiatives in the community where he lives and beyond.

Today, after volunteering for over 15 months; he is the Executive Director of New Neighbor Relief – NNR (www.newneighborrelief.org) in San Diego, California and the President of the Congolese Family Support Organization (CFSO).

APPENDIX: NEW NEIGHBOR RELIEF – NNR CORNER

This is a 501(c)3 nonprofit organization working to help refugees in their long and difficult journey to start a new life in the United States. In the San Diego area it is attempting to find positive solutions to problems discussed in this book.

New Neighbor Relief – NNR partners with resettlement agencies in San Diego as a support to serve as a bridge between these organizations and the refuges as soon as they are resettled in the area.

New Neighbor Relief (NNR) is not a competitor to the existing resettlement agencies. It works rather as a support to resettlement agencies. The great incentive is to contribute by filling the gaps in their efforts for better service provision to refugee families using NNR stronghold strategies, with committed, loving and caring team to do so.

- **Mission and vision statements**
  a. **Mission**

    To lovingly assist and mentor refugees and asylum seekers with economic, social, and educational needs so they become self-reliant and able to contribute to the development of their families and communities.

  b. **Vision**

    To become the most reliable organization helping refugees and asylum seekers become contributors and assets in their new society.

- **Difference between NNR and other agencies**

There is a biggest difference between NNR and other agencies working with refugees in San Diego and this difference is part of the main reasons why NNR was formed after finding the need to do more in assisting refugees in our community. The difference is explained by the facts that:

- The organization has a large number of enthusiastic volunteers who understand the problems refugees face and volunteer their time out of love rather than a job.
- The majority of the administrative costs of the organization are covered by the Board of Directors, therefore most of the donated funds go directly to the cause.
- The organization deals with refugee matters in a very responsive manner so that problems don't become greater.
- NNR answers refugee calls 24/7.
- NNR team spends more time in the field and less time in the office.
- The Board of Directors are individuals who care more about people than their own social status.

- **Working with other support agencies**

"New Neighbor Relief (NNR)" works in partnership with other refugee support agencies for a better intervention. The organization is already working with Alliance for African Assistance, Catholic Charities, International Rescue Committee (IRC) and Jewish Family Service San Diego as agencies sponsoring refugee resettlement in the United States of America (USA) and in San Diego particularly. NNR is also in consultation with different churches to reach the neediest refugee families as well as many informal organizations such as Parents-Students-Refugee-Organization (PSRO), Syrian Refugee community among others.

NNR works with agencies sponsoring refugees' resettlement in San Diego to help them expedite assistance in the transition period between the resettlement time and the access to government services (welfare). Once a refugee family or individual has been resettled is San Diego, "New Neighbor Relief" goes through an evaluation process with the assigned family to determine the immediate needs and future needs. After the evaluation has been completed, a prequalified volunteer mentor individual(s) or family will be assigned to help the refugee family according to the plan given to the mentor by the organization leaders.

Program outline

"New Neighbor Relief (NNR)" is a seeking to help refugees transition into a new life in America by helping them become self-reliant. NNR has adopted three (3) core programs to help with this effort:

1. **Language:** Learning English will help refugees gain employment or further their education. Our English program has 3 components, which separates us from the traditional ESL:
   - "Literacy Program" to help those who are illiterate in their native language.
   - "How to Teach English" is an ESL program that uses creative techniques to help refugees acquire skills quickly.
   - "Daily Dose Program" which is an in-home conversational English subprogram to help refugees practice English at home. This is done with mentors or any other volunteer teachers who subscribe with NNR for such activities. It is very helpful because refugees who are enrolled in ESL classes don't practice English at home.

2. **Employment**: Getting a job is the single most important way for refugees to become self-reliant. NNR helps with employment by assisting them with:
   - Creating resumes
   - Developing skills in finding a job
   - Supplying referrals for potential jobs
   - Training on work ethics

3. **Transportation**: Transportation is a key element in helping refugees become independent and NNR helps in the following ways:
   - Help with acquiring a bus pass or bicycle
   - Assist with preparing for the driving permit test and driver's license test
   - Help purchase an automobile that is adequate for their job and family
   - Teach them about maintenance, insurance, and safety

Apart from the 3 core programs, NNR runs a Mentorship Program, which assigns a mentor family to a refugee family. They serve in line with the Vision and Mission of the organization.

Through the resources allocated by NNR, the mentor family can assist the refugee family with:

- **Food**: NNR can help refugees with food when cash or food stamps have depleted.
- **Emergency Fund**: NNR have an emergency fund set aside to help refugees with rent, utilities, and other vital expenses.
- **Transportation**: On occasion NNR or mentor family help refugees with transportation to and from doctor's appointments, resettlement appointments, English classes (when needed), stores, churches (for those who go to church), etc.
- **Medication**: NNR provides over-the-counter medication that refugee families so often need such as Ibuprofen, Children's Tylenol, cold medicine, Band-Aids, and eye drops.
- **Clothing and Household items**: NNR has a warehouse of donations consisting of clothing, shoes, and household items that are available to all refugees.

*Mentors are not expected nor permitted to assist refugees with cash or commodities.

More information regarding this organization including the different ways to get involved can be found on the website www.newneighborrelief.org

ABBREVIATIONS

AIDS:	Acquired Immune Deficiency Syndrome
AIU:	Atlantic International University
CEFEVO:	Comité d'Encadrement des Femmes et des Enfants – Veuves Orphelins
CFSO:	Congolese Family Support Organization
CFSSC:	Congolese Family Support Steering Committee.
COFAS:	Conseil des Organization de Femmes Assissant en Synergie
CW:	CalWorks
DV:	Domestic Violence
DMV:	Department of Motor Vehicles
DRC:	Democratic Republic of Congo
ESE:	Expended Subsidized work Experience
ESL:	English as a Second Language
IOM:	International Organization for Migration
IRC:	International Rescue Committee
HIV:	Human Immunodeficiency Virus
LARC:	Language Acquisition Resource Centre
MISP:	Minimum Initial Services Package
MPM:	Masters of Project Management
n.d:	No date
NNR:	New Neighbor Relief
NSDI:	Nile Sisters Development Initiative
PCG:	Public Consult Group
PTSD:	Post Traumatic Stress Disorder
RCA:	Refugee Cash Aid
RIP:	Rest In Peace
RTM:	Refugee Transitional Maintenance

SDRF: San Diego Refugee Forum
SDSU: San Diego State University
SRH: Sexual and Reproductive Health
UNDP: United Nations Development Program
UNFAO: United Nations Food and Agriculture Organization
UNFPA: United Nations Population Fund
UNHCR: United Nations High Commission for Refugees
UNWFP: United Nations World Food Program
UNICEF: United Nations Children's Fund
UNWHO: United Nations World Health Organization
USA: United States of America
USCIS: United States Citizenship and Immigration Services
US: United States
WEX: Work Experience
WF: Wilson Fish

REFERENCES

Altshuler, M, Scott, K, & Carevya, B. (2011). Acculturation and health. Refugee Health. Retrieved from
http://refugeehealthta.org/prevention-and-wellness/acculturation-and-health/

Brouwer, K, C, & Rodwell, T. (2007). Assessment of community member attitudes towards health needs of refugees in San Diego.

Burks, M. (2014). The Three Big Issues Facing San Diego's Refugee Community. Voice of San Diego. Retrieved 2 August 2017, from
http://www.voiceofsandiego.org/topics/news/the-three-big-issues-facing-san-diegosrefugee-community/

Burks, M. (2014). San Diego's Richest Poor Neighborhood, Two Decades Later. Voice of San Diego. Retrieved 2 August 2017, from
http://www.voiceofsandiego.org/topics/news/san-diegos-richest-poor-neighborhood-two-decades-later/

Cohen, S. (2009). The reproductive health needs of refugees and displaced people: an opening for renewed US leadership. Guttmacher Policy Review, 12(3), 15-19.

Corcoran, A. (August 2017). Refugee resettlement is driven by a desire for cheap compliant labor, not humanitarianism. Retrieved from
https://refugeeresettlementwatch.wordpress.com/2017/08/02/refugee-resettlement-is-driven-by-a-desire-for-cheap-compliant-labor-not-humanitarianism/

Garrett, K. E. (2006). Living in America: Challenges facing new immigrants and refugees. Princeton Township, NJ: Robert Wood Johnson Foundation.

Gushulak, B. D., Weekers, J., & MacPherson, D. W. (2009). Migrants and emerging public health issues in a globalized world: threats, risks and challenges, an evidence-based framework. Emerging Health Threats Journal, 2(1), 7091.

Hope for San Diego. (n.d). Welcoming the stranger. Retrieved 29 July 2017, from http://hopeforsd.org/refugeesandimmigrants/

Hynes, T. (2003). New issues in refugee research. The issue of 'trust'or 'mistrust'in research with refugees: choices, caveats and considerations for researchers.

Geneva: Evaluation and Policy Analysis Unit, The United Nations Refugee Agency.

International Rescue Committee. (2017). Seven common myths about refugee resettlement in the United States. Retrieved 29 July 2017, from https://www.rescue.org/article/seven-common-myths-about-refugee-resettlement united-states

Kesselly, L. (2002). Focusing on older refugees. Forced Migration Review, 14, 17-18.

Leaning, J., Spiegel, P., & Crisp, J. (2011). Public health equity in refugee situations. Conflict and health, 5(1), 6.

McCarthy, K. (1998). Adaptation of immigrant children to the United States: A review of the literature. Center for Research on Child Wellbeing: Working Paper, 98(03). Morris, M. D., Popper, S. T., Rodwell, T. C., Brodine, S. K., & Brouwer, K. C. (2009).

Healthcare barriers of refugees' post-resettlement. Journal of community health, 34(6), 529.

NISKANEN Center. (March, 2017). Overview of Refugee Resettlement in the United States. Retrieved 29 July 2017, from https://niskanencenter.org/wpcontent/uploads/2017/03/OverviewofRefugeeR esettlentintheUnitedStatesPolicyBrief-1-1.pdf

Nunez, C. (2014). The 7 biggest challenges facing refugees and immigrants in the US. Global Citizen. Retrieved from https://www.globalcitizen.org/en/content/the-7-biggest-challenges-facing-refugeesand-iimmig/

Parvini, S. (2017). A hub for Iraqi refugees, San Diego is making way for new faces-this time from Syria. Los Angeles Times. Retrieved from

http://www.latimes.com/local/california/la-me-syrian-refugees-el-cajon-20170213-story.html

Refugee Council U.S.A. (January, 2017). Refugee resettlement in the United States. Retrieved 29 July 2017, from https://static1.squarespace.com/static/577d437bf5e231586a7055a9/t/5881079 b20099ec2c4c010c9/1484851100541/Refugee+Resettlement+Backgrounder+-+January+2017.pdf

Sanchez, T. (2015). County tops in refugee resettlement. The San Diego Union Tribune. Retrieved 3 August 2017, from http://www.sandiegouniontribune.com/news/immigration/sdut-refugees-re-settle-syria-iraq-chaldean-saigon-2015oct07-htmlstory.html

Schorshit, N. (March 2017). Despite Inclusive Policies, Refugee Children Face Major Obstacles to Education. Retrieved from http://neatoday.org/2017/03/21/refugee-students-facing-major-obstacles-to-education/

Sowey, H. (2005). Are refugees at increased risk of substance misuse? Sydney:Drug and Alcohol Multicultural Education Centre.

Spracklin, P. (2017). The Top 10 Problems Faced by Immigrants. IMMI

Group. Retrieved from
https://www.immigroup.com/news/top-10-problems-immigrants

UNHCR. (2016). Missing out: Refugee education in crisis. Retrieved from
http://uis.unesco.org/sites/default/files/documents/missing-out-refugee-edu-cation-in-crisis_unhcr_2016-en.pdf

UNHCR. (n.d). Resettlement in the United States. Retrieved 29 July 2017,
from http://www.unhcr.org/resettlement-in-the-united-states.html

UNHCR. (n.d). Reproductive Health. Retrieved 3 August 2017, from
http://www.unhcr.org/reproductive-health.html

U.S Department of State. (n.d). Retrieved 29 July 2017, from
https://www.state.gov/j/prm/ra/

U.S Citizenship and Immigration Services. (2016). The United States Refugee
Admissions Program (USRAP) Consultation & Worldwide Processing Prior-ities. Retrieved 3 July 2017, from
https://www.uscis.gov/humanitarian/refugees-asylum/refugees/united-states-refugee-admissions-program-usrap-consultation-worldwide-processing-priorities

Zong, j & Batalova, J. (2017). Refugees and Asylums in the United States. Mi-gration Policy Institute. Retrieved from 3 August 2017 from
http://www.migrationpolicy.org/article/refugees-and-asylees-united-states/

ADDENDUM

African countries where Swahili is spoken

The map below shows the parts of Africa where Swahili Language is spoken:

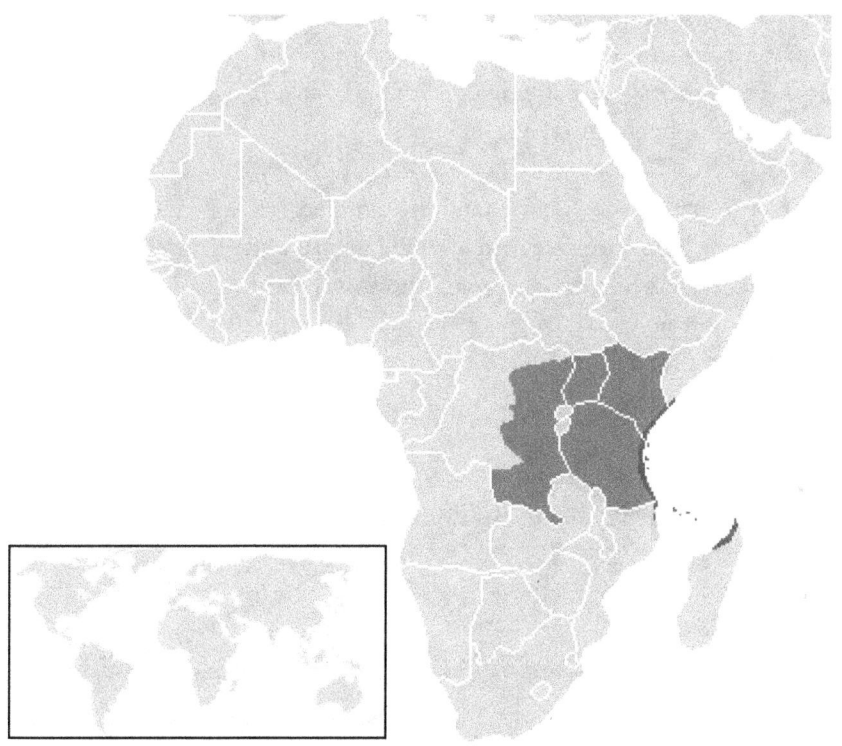

Short list of Swahili vocabulary variations

Unlike other refugees in San Diego, California, refugees from the Democratic Republic of Congo (DRC) who speak Swahili language suffer from a "double language barrier". First, they have problems with English language because they come from a country which uses French as an official language. Second, they suffer from barriers of Swahili language because this language is in conflict with itself. The Swahili language spoken in DR Congo (also known as Kingwana) is different from the Swahili language spoken in East African countries (Kenya, Tanzania…).

For instance, a refugee from Iraq who is Arabic speaking will use the help of an interpreter/translator to access services in San Diego, California whereas a refugee from the Democratic Republic of Congo (DRC) will need to use the help of an interpreter/translator but he/she will not understand what the interpreter/translator is saying if the latter is from East African (Kenya, Tanzania) because they speak a different dialect of the same language in which many words are absolutely different.

In order to help readers understand this problem, I came up with this short list of sample differences between Swahili Language and Kingwana. In this list I focused more on the words commonly used by providers in healthcare setting to try to show how these language barriers can put refugees' lives at risk (of death) when they are sick.

Some Swahili variations list

Swahil (as spoken in East Africa – Kenya and Tanzania)	In Kingwana a Swahili "dialect" (as spoken in Central Africa – DR Congo)	Meaning in English
	Day of the week	
Juma pili	Siku ya Mungu	Sunday
Juma tatu	Siku ya kwanza	Monday
Jumanne	Siku ya pili	Tuesday
Juma tano	Siku ya tatu	Wednesday
Alhamisi	Siku ya ine	Thursday
Ijumaa	Siku ya tano	Friday
Jumamosi	Siku ya sita (siku ya posho)	Saturday
	Numbers (Counting)	
Ishirini	Makumi mbili	Twenty
Thelathini	Makumi tatu	Thirty
Arobaini	Makumi ine	Forty
Hamsini	Makumi tano	Fifty
Sitini	Makumi sita	Sixty
Sabini	Makumi saba	Seventy
Thema nini	Makumi munane	Eighty
Tisini	Makumi kenda	Ninety
Tisa	Kenda	Nine
	Human body parts	
Jaw	Chafu	Jaw
Cheek	Machafu	Cheek
Chin	Kidevu	Chin
Jicho	Licho	Eye
Sikio	Lisikio	Ear
Pua	Mapua	Nose
Mouth	Kiywa	Mouth
Mecho	Macho	Teeth
Ulimi	Lulimi	Tongue
Titi	Liziba	Breast
Kitovu	Kitofu	Navel
Mguu	Mugulu	Leg
Kifua	Kiwiliwili/Kifuwa	Chest
Nyele	Nywele	Hair
Tofaa ya Adam	Kameza bugali	Adam's apple
Matumbo	Butumbutumbu	Intestines
Ini	Maini	Liver
Mapafu	Mafafa	Lungs
Ubongo	Bongo	Brain
Goti	Ligoti	Knee
Miguu	Migulu	Feet

Note: In the table above, I focused on some vocabulary words which are commonly used in healthcare setting with the purpose of showing how dangerous it can be for East African interpreters/translators to interpret or translate for refugees from the Democratic Republic of Congo (DRC) living in San Diego or other parts of the Unites States. I shall come up with more vocabulary words in a Swahili (Kingwana) interpreter/translator handbook that I am preparing as another contribution to solving this problem.

English or French words which have no meaning in Swahili are always replaced by the same words either in English or in French depending upon whether the speaker is from central Africa (DR Congo) or from East Africa (Tanzania or Kenya).

I am planning to conduct a research to find out about a list of words in Farsi language as well to be included in our forthcoming interpreter/translator handbook... this will be possible only if I find some financial support because I will need other people to be involved in the research.